Social Change in the
Capitalist World Economy

POLITICAL ECONOMY OF THE WORLD-SYSTEM ANNUALS

Series Editor: IMMANUEL WALLERSTEIN

Published in cooperation with the Section on the Political Economy of the World-System of the American Sociological Association.

About the Series

The intent of this series of annuals is to reflect and inform the intense theoretical and empirical debates about the "political economy of the world-system." These debates assume that the phenomena of the real world cannot be separated into three (or more) categories—political, economic, and social—which can be studied by different methods and in closed spheres. The economy is "institutionally" rooted; the polity is the expression of socioeconomic forces; and "societal" structures are a consequence of politico-economic pressures. The phrase "world-system" also tells us that we believe there is a working social system larger than any state whose operations are themselves a focus of social analysis. How states and parties, firms and classes, status groups and social institutions operate within the framework and constraints of the world-system is precisely what is debated.

These theme-focused annuals will be the outlet for original theoretical and empirical findings of social scientists coming from all the traditional "disciplines." The series will draw upon papers presented at meetings and conferences, as well as papers from those who share in these concerns.

Volumes in this series:

Volume 1: *Social Change in the Capitalist World Economy* (1978)
Barbara Hockey Kaplan, *Editor*

Social Change in the Capitalist World Economy

Edited by
Barbara Hockey Kaplan

Volume 1, **Political Economy of the World-System Annuals**
Series Editor: Immanuel Wallerstein

 SAGE Publications   Beverly Hills / London

For information address:

SAGE PUBLICATIONS, INC.
275 South Beverly Drive
Beverly Hills, California 90212

SAGE PUBLICATIONS LTD
28 Banner Street
London EC1Y 8QE

Printed in the United States of America

International Standard Book Number 0-8039-1032-0 (cloth)
International Standard Book Number 0-8039-1033-9 (paper)

Library of Congress Catalog Card No. 78-50825

FIRST PRINTING

CONTENTS

PART FOUR: WORLD SYSTEM ANALYSIS: THEORETICAL AND METHODOLOGICAL ISSUES

PREFACE

The phrase "political economy of the world-system" dates from the 1970s. It is, however, an old concern, one that was well developed in the last third of the 19th century up to the end of World War I. The writings of Mahan, Hobson, and Lenin, of Bukharin and Schumpeter, even in an indirect way of Weber, were all centered around this topic, if under various appelations. Then for various reasons, these concerns receded, to be renewed more recently. What are these concerns, and why have they moved in and out of the forefront of intellectual analysis?

The very words of the phrase indicate the assumptions involved. "Political economy" tells us that we are assuming that meaningful analysis cannot separate the phenomena of the real world into three (or more) categories—the political, the economic, the social—to be studied by different methods and in closed spheres (even momentarily). The economy is "institutionally" rooted; the polity is the expression of socioeconomic forces; "societal" structures are a consequence of politico-economic pressures.

"World-system" tells us that we believe there is a working social system larger than any state whose operations are themselves a focus (for many, the primordial focus) of social analysis. How states and parties, firms and classes, status groups and social institutions operate within the framework and constraints of the world-system is precisely what is debated.

Those who write about the "political economy of the world-system" share these two premises. Beyond that, however, one finds intense debates—both theoretical and empirical—which it is the intent of this series of annuals to reflect.

Why these analytic concerns move forward and back on the stage of scholarship is a question that itself requires research. My hunch is that it is not accidental that both the present concern and the previous one arose during the period when the first signs of relative decline of a hegemonic world power were evident. These "first signs" are in many ways very intellectually upsetting, ending a period of consensual "certainty," and forcing analysts to raise questions precisely about the largest framework of social action itself. As for the receding of concern in the 1920s, I hesitate to express even a guess.

These theme-focused annuals will be the outlet for original theoretical and empirical findings of social scientists coming from all the so-called "disciplines," who have agreed to meet in an annual conference to be held in the United States. It is an open circle for all those who share our concern.

Immanuel Wallerstein
Series Editor

Binghamton, N.Y.
December, 1977

INTRODUCTION

Barbara Hockey Kaplan

As a collection, these papers reflect and refract the recent work of Immanuel Wallerstein not only in research and writing but in founding a "school" in world system studies. In reporting their authors' work in progress, they do much more than this. They present some of the latest findings of extensive research on world capitalism. At the same time, from a range of theoretical and political perspectives, all deal with Wallerstein's model of the capitalist world economy and his method of studying it. So, beyond the sum of its parts, this collection may serve as a prism for viewing Wallerstein's "modern world system" through the applications of those who accept it as it stands, others' attempts at modification, and some case studies which pose challenges to its defining characteristics.

The Modern World-System (Wallerstein, 1974a) won the Sorokin Award for 1975 of the American Sociological Association. Building on the work of the dependency theorists as well as that of the French "Annales" school, notably Fernand Braudel, this study of the origins and emergence of the capitalist world economy was greeted as a breakthrough in United States sociology. The announcement of the award at the ASA annual meetings in San Francisco added impetus to the efforts of Wallerstein, and most of the authors represented here, to form an association section on the political economy of the world system.

"Modernization: requiescat in pace" (Wallerstein, 1974b) was the title of Wallerstein's paper at the meetings in which he symbolically laid to rest the dominant paradigm for the study of "development," disinterred the problem and perspective of classical social studies, and presented an agenda for those who would understand and thus contribute to the world-systemic transition from capitalism to socialism.

Here is the agenda, quoted extensively to provide the focus of this collection. It also conveys best the sense of Wallerstein charging ahead of the field on one of Hobsbawm's horses which "can be recognized and ridden by those who can't define them."[1] Wallerstein first stressed that we live in a capitalist not a "modernizing" world, then hammered home his main point—the very essence of his perspective—that we need to study as a whole the world system where, for the first time, "the entire game is resumed in the internal relations, . . . of core to periphery, of bourgeois to proletarian, of hegemonic culture to cultures of resistance, of dominant strata . . . to institutionally oppressed racial and ethnic strata, of the party of order to the party of movement." He then outlined five major arenas for research:

1. . . . the internal functioning of the capitalist world-economy as a system; the institutional ways in which areas get located at the core, the periphery and the semi-periphery of that system, and how units can and do change their location; the mechanisms of transfers of surplus towards the core; the ways in which classes emerge, consolidate and disintegrate; the multiple expressions of class struggle; the creation, sustenance and destruction of all varieties of "status-groups" (ethno-national groups, racial castes, age and sex groups), and the ways these "status" groupings interweave with class structure; the cultural expressions of conflicting interests; the pattern of interplay between cyclical processes of expansion and contraction and the secular evolutionary processes that undermine the basic stability of the system; the modalities of, and resistances to the proletarianization of labor and the commercialization of land; the role of the state in affecting the world market and aiding specific groups within it; the rise of anti-systemic revolutionary movements.

2. . . . how and when the capitalist world-economy was created in the first place; why the transition took place in Europe and not elsewhere; why it took place when it did and not earlier or later.

3. . . . For at least three centuries (the 16th to the 18th) the capitalist world economy functioned side by side with non-capitalist social systems. . . . How did it relate to them? . . . what were the processes that made it possible for the capitalist world-economy to incorporate them?

4. . . . comparative study of the various historical forms of the social system, the alternative modes of production (three up to now): . . . reciprocal, . . . redistributive, . . . the capitalist (market) mode found in world economies.

5. . . . the fourth system based on a socialist mode of production, our future world government. . . . We must look afresh at the various "socialist" experiences, seen as regimes that are both seeking to transform the world-system and partially to prefigure the future one, . . . the relationship of revolutionary movements . . . of the world-system to each other. [Wallerstein, 1976; 133-135]

Wallerstein's prize and paper, as well as others presented at the world system section meetings, stimulated work on many parts of this agenda. Scholars and small programs, hitherto isolated, were brought into contact with the section's founding members and their work. At American University in Washington, D.C., the sociology department organized a conference on it. When the ASA organizing section met again at the next annual meetings in 1976 in New York, its members decided to hold annual section meetings between the national association meetings, and that the first of these meetings would be the American University conference. The First Annual Spring Conference on the Political Economy of the World System took place in Washington on March 31 and April 1, 1977. It is the papers presented at the conference which are collected here. The authors reported and discussed their work in progress. Some of it, clearly, is still incomplete. The purpose was, and is, to stimulate and guide further work in this field. Conference sessions were arranged around papers which could be clustered more or less coherently. That organization is retained here.

The speakers were not asked to address Wallerstein's work specifically. Although all the papers relate to it, how they do so is usually made explicit only for the specific issues each raises.

Even here, much is left implicit. So the set of papers taken together do not convey, even in broadest outlines, Wallerstein's analysis of "the determining elements of the modern world-system." Nor is a summary account of it to be found in his book. Wallerstein does, however, give this synopsis of the scope of his study:

> This first volume deals with the origins and early conditions of the world-system, still only a European world-system. The approximate dates of this are 1450-1640. The second volume shall deal with the consolidation of this system, roughly between 1640 and 1815. The third shall deal with the conversion of the world economy into a global enterprise, made possible by the technical transformation of modern industrialism. This expansion was so sudden and so great that the system in effect had to be recreated. The period here is roughly 1815-1917. The fourth volume will deal with the consolidation of this capitalist world-economy from 1917 to the present, and the particular "revolutionary" tensions this consolidation has provoked. [1974a:10-11]

The theoretical model used to explain all this is not presented in the first volume. It is still being explicated in a series of articles of which the most comprehensive is "The rise and future demise of the world capitalist system: concepts for comparative analysis" (Wallerstein, 1974b).

The most succinct and lucid account of Wallerstein's model of the world system is that of Theda Skocpol in her critique of his book. She abstracts from it, of course, for her own analytical purposes, but here summary of the model includes those parts with which she and Ellen Kay Trimberger take issue in their paper as well as much of what we need in approaching the other papers in this volume:

> Wallerstein insists that any theory of social change must refer to a "social system"—that is, a "largely self-contained" entity whose developmental dynamics are "largely internal" (1974a: 347). For self-containment to obtain, he reasons, the entity in question must be based upon a complete economic division of labor. Leaving aside small-scale, isolated subsistence economies, there have been, he says, only two kinds of large-scale social

systems: (1) empires, in which a functional economic division of labor, occupationally not geographically based, is subsumed under an overarching, tribute-collecting imperial state, and

(2) world economies, in which there are multiple political sovereignties, no one of which can subsume and control the entire economic system. A world economy should be, in Wallerstein's view, more able than a world empire to experience sustained economic development precisely because economic actors have more freedom to maneuver and to appropriate and reinvest surpluses.

Such a world economy—of which capitalism from the sixteenth century to the present has been (according to Wallerstein) the only long-lasting historical instance—is based upon a geographically differentiated division of labor, featuring three main zones—core, semiperiphery and periphery—tied together by world market trade in bulk commodities that are necessary for everyday consumption. Each major zone of the world economy has an economic structure based upon its particular mixture of economic activities (e.g., industry plus differentiated agriculture in the core; monoculture in the periphery) and its characteristic form of "labor control" (e.g., skilled wage labor and tenantry in the core; sharecropping in the semiphery; and slavery or "coerced cash-crop labor" in the periphery). The different zones are differentially rewarded by the world economy, with surplus flowing disproportionately to the core areas. Moreover, the economic structure of each zone supports a given sort of dominant class oriented toward the world market, as well as states of a certain strength (strongest in the core and weakest in the periphery) that operate in the interests of that class. Finally, according to Wallerstein, the differential strength of the multiple states within the world capitalist economy is crucial for maintaining the system as a whole, for the strong states reinforce and increase the differential flow of surplus to the core zone. This happens because strong states can provide "extraeconomic" assistance to allow their capitalist classes to manipulate and enforce terms of trade in their favor on the world market. [Skocpol, 1977:1076-1077]

Here we begin to see how Wallerstein relates the elements of his listed agenda in his explanation of the emergence, persistence, and eventual decline of world capitalism. It was here, too, that the major issues in the conference began to emerge. The purposes of the participants as well as the problems they had been studying were in general accord with Wallerstein's agenda. It was about his model and method that questions were raised, more or less explicitly and more by some speakers than others. The questions concerned the model's level of generality versus historical specificity; those parts of it, such as the world market, given logical primacy; the relation between important elements, such as states and dominant classes; and, of course, whether these and other aspects of it limit its usefulness for the task for which Wallerstein has developed it—the study of a specific case of social change—the "rise and future demise" of world capitalism.

It is here that the limitation of the scope of the conference to work being done related to this perspective offers an advantage that even the more trenchant of the purely theoretical critiques of Wallerstein's work cannot. It traces in more detail the implications of his formulation when confronted with historical phenomena studied extensively by these authors. The advantage is greatest when the authors move with relative ease among the different dimensions of this kind of work: from metatheory to theorizing, from the analytical to the historical, from macroscopic to fine-grained analysis.

The studies on which they are drawing to discuss the use and usefulness of the world system perspective are not developed within that perspective alone. Most of them rest firmly on Marxist work done in recent decades as well as that of Marx himself. Wallerstein is addressing Marx's problem—the dynamics of capitalism—using some of Marx's concepts within a new theoretical argument and retaining others while changing their meaning, their denotation. His "mode of production" is not that of Marx. The more explicitly and self-consciously the other writers locate their own work within the Marxist tradition or in relation to it, the more useful are their papers for assessing the specific merits of this new perspective in explaining world capitalism in its present phase. This is equally true for the different kinds of structuralism which inform some of this work.

Fred Block, in the first paper on theories of the state in Marxist analysis, explores the implications of adding the world system perspective, which he takes to be structuralist, onto Marxist theory with its emphasis on the relation of class consciousness and structural forces and constraints. He sees, as have earlier critics, that the result is not dialectical synthesis but analytical confusion. But Block goes on to wrestle with the fit of the two theories by narrowing the issue to that of relations between class and state and from class consciousness to "intentionality." This, in the world system perspective, becomes an international strategic consciousness on the part of capitalists in core states. He can then suggest ways of studying whether and how this influences the policies implemented by state managers. It is a useful test of fit because it forces recognition of *specific* problems of evidence and inference. Skocpol and Trimberger, working with a different conception of class-state relations, use a similar approach. They introduce and acknowledge Marx's analysis where it is relevant to their problem, specify what they are retaining of it, what they are modifying and how. Their use of world system concepts is equally explicit and systematic. (These two papers also take into account, theoretically, the role of the producing class in bringing about social change. Whether this is fortuitous or due to a more systematic attempt at synthesizing Marxist and world system theory, it is rather rare in the latter where the view is more generally from above, from the level of the dominant class of powerful states.) Whether or not class intentionality may still be influencing state policy, perhaps from within the state, and whether or not Trimberger's revolutions would be recognized as such by Marx and others of us, these authors show us how to go about conceptualizing specific problems in terms of a systematic theoretical argument so that they can be explained not just historically—*post hoc ergo propter hoc*—or teleologically, but theoretically.

Other authors try various ways around this problem of synthesizing a Marxist world system analysis. Douglas Dowd emphasizes Wallerstein's method of addressing a complex array of elements of a world system whose complexity increases its stability. He urges a more flexible application of Marx's method if we are to understand capitalism's capacity to endure, strengthened by the very contradictions which should have brought it down. He notes the difference in their models of capitalism, which affects its periodization by a couple of centuries, but does not dwell on this. Samih K. Farsoun and Walter F. Carroll stay close to Marx and reduce the world system perspective to a "contextual variable" in their analysis.

Christopher Chase-Dunn and Wallerstein both avoid some of the thornier issues of the dynamics of social change in the two theoretical perspectives. Movement in Chase-Dunn's model is oscillation, a "circulation of elites" of hegemonic powers related to alternation in their relations with the periphery as well as to the long waves of capitalist expansion and contraction. Wallerstein presents a model wherein what was structure is now process, where there is no proletariat and no bourgeoisie but proletarianization and bourgeoisification in a world system expanding by peripheralization. Elsewhere Wallerstein has discussed his added geographic dimension in class relations in his system, that of his zones. Areas move up from the periphery to the core as well as in to it.

Richard Rubinson, in the second paper, "Political Transformation in Germany and the United States," explores national development from the world system perspective, by which he means this movement of national states toward the core, and the conditions which allow it to occur. In exploring the relative strength and the struggle for power of the Junkers and the industrialists in Germany, and the southern planters and the industrialists in the United States, he finds world system class relations and economic conditions, notably those of Britain, the hegemonic power in the period he studies, as crucial in enabling the political coalitions formed by these German and United States groups to develop into solid political and economic alliances. These alliances, together with the external conditions allowing for the possibility of development, move both Germany and the United States toward the core.

Walter L. Goldfrank, like Rubinson, is concerned with demonstrating the usefulness of the world system perspective in shedding new light on well studied history, by reordering it as well as relating new material to that already studied. Both papers are less concerned with the problems of synthesis discussed earlier but their accounts are so detailed as to afford us an opportunity to evaluate the merits of this kind of synthetic reworking.

Goldfrank's paper on "Fascism and World Economy" is another using, as its main categories, Wallerstein's core, semiperiphery, and periphery. Goldfrank, too, is concerned with nation state competition for movement toward the core or hegemony within it and, like Chase-Dunn, he discusses the timing of hegemonic shifts and the economic contraction of capital which he relates to the rise of fascism. For Goldfrank, this interstate competition and capital accumulation are together the sources of dynamism in the world system perspective. He has studied fascism, with its appeal to the nation as the primary focus of loyalty, as the nexus of class and national forces. Using Wallerstein's three zones and his own typology of stages of fascism, Goldfrank attempts to integrate and modify the analysis and findings of two sets of theoretical studies of fascism, one set liberal, the other Marxist, Block's caveat notwithstanding. This enables him to make differential predictions, or "comparative observations" of the present and immediate future with the interwar period, on the likely emergence or resurgence of fascism in the three zones. His explicit inclusion of the future is rare in these discussions of movement and timing within the world system.

It is in the next paper by Skocpol and Trimberger, "Revolutions and the World-Historical Development of Capitalism: Some Hypotheses," that we come closer to the study of change as social transformation. Wallerstein set this as the problem for his study, and presumably for world system studies, in the opening lines of his book: "Unless we are to use the study of social change as a term synonymous to the totality of social science, its meaning should be restricted to the study of changes in those phenomena which are most durable . . . great structural changes . . . that make the world of today qualitatively different from the world of yesterday" (1974a:3).

Skocpol and Trimberger address this problem in their comparative historical studies of social revolutions in France, Russia, and China, and bureaucratic revolutions from above in Japan and Turkey. They argue, against Wallerstein's position in other writings, that national revolutions which abolish capitalist private property and institute state ownership and control of the means of production do make a real difference for the structure, dynamics, and longevity of the world capitalist system. The restrictions they place on international capital investment and trade disrupt capitalism even if pressures from the capitalist world economy and the international state system hinder the further change to sociopolitical equality within and between nations.

This analysis by Skocpol and Trimberger of the role of internal class and political struggle and consequent equalitarian tendencies in "state socialist" revolutions extends that of Marx which gives central importance to class struggle in revolution, that is, social transformation. Like Marx, they conceive of capitalism as a mode of production based upon the relation between wage labor and capital but also, with Wallerstein, as a world economy with interdependent zones. They diverge from both in their conceptual emphasis, similar to that of Perry Anderson, on the international system of states neither originally created by capitalism nor reducible to it.

There may be another, more general, difference between these authors and Wallerstein. They may, as Terence Hopkins suggests in a later paper, be doing a different kind of historical sociology.

In their paper, "State Capitalism and Counterrevolution in the Middle East," Farsoun and Carroll report part of their continuing study of the Arab periphery of the capitalist world economy. They focus on state capitalism as a mode of production and stress as crucial the integrated analysis of national and class issues. They see the related national and class issues as the sources of contradictions which determine the counterrevolutionary character of state capitalist regimes, which originated as anti-imperialist national liberation movements.

Although they are working on the interweaving of ethno-national groupings and class structure listed in Wallerstein's

San Francisco agenda, and although it was Walter Carroll who suggested that the American University sociology department organize this conference on the world system, their work has been influenced more by Petras than Wallerstein. As noted earlier, they diverge sharply from Wallerstein in treating the world system as a contextual variable in their analysis, albeit an important one. Also they challenge the level of abstraction, both spatial and temporal, of his conceptualization. They suggest that a better way to develop theory in this historical materialist context is by the use of successive approximations based on studies of historical situations specific enough to indicate explicitly the class struggles they contain. Here they are closer to Skocpol and Trimberger. Of all the authors, they are at present most directly involved in the processes they are reporting and in studying them at first hand.

Where Farsoun and Carroll have been concerned with political processes in the immediate present, Chase-Dunn, in his paper, is working at an abstract level of model building. Where their perspective is distant from that of Wallerstein, even in some ways opposed to it, his is very close. His paper contains an account of Wallerstein's conception, which he shares, of a capitalist mode of production, and specifically capitalist relations of production in contradistinction to that of Marx. Their emphasis is on the continuing role of primitive accumulation in modern world capitalism. This entails what Wallerstein calls "mixed modes of labor control," which he touches upon in his paper.

Chase-Dunn, who has been working with Rubinson on a structural approach to the world system, presents a structural model, which he proposes to test later, of the effects of changes in the distribution of economic power among core states on the structure and control of exchange between the core and the periphery. The model is complex and includes also the rate of aggregate economic growth of the world economy as a whole, the level of political and military conflict between core powers, expansion and deepening of economic exploitation of the periphery, expansion of colonial empires and the development of peripheral resistance to the core. The final element has not

been given much attention by Wallerstein although it is important for his theoretical account of the role of the semi-periphery.

Dowd's part in the program was different from the rest and
aroused the greatest audience response, both positive and
negative. His talk was a "trou normand" in the rather heavy
conceptual repast the audience was by then trying to digest.
The lone economist among these sociologists, his was the
mellowed Marxism of one who had continued its teaching in the
United States during the Cold War. He reminded us that Marx,
our fellow social scientist, space and time bound then as we are
now, did not and could not set himself to explain the problems
of world capitalism we now confront. We must understand and
apply Marxian concepts with greater flexibility and imagination
as well as endless historical study if we are to help make socialism
more than a possibility. In his paper, "Continuity, Change,
and Tension in Global Capitalism," Dowd examines, in ways
stimulated by Wallerstein, "certain aspects of capitalist history
. . . to try to show how the weakness or strength of the accumulation process has allowed contradictions to generate destructive
or yield therapeutic social changes." He stresses the historical
fact that they have done as much to strengthen capitalism as to
undermine it particularly in the period since Marx, where the
deepening contradictions are "shallowed" as they are spread
throughout the world system. Dowd's own understanding and
application of the concept of contradiction derives from Marx's
analysis of the dynamics of capital and is quite different from
Wallerstein's usage of the term.

The relation of concept to theory is one of the problems
Hopkins mentions in his paper on methodological issues in
world system analysis. They are problems which arise in working
within a new perspective which means in a philosophical and,
thus, logical tradition other than that in which we have been
educated and which is all-pervasive in our society. What we have
to unlearn, specifically, is what has loosely been called positivism
and, within that, the discipline of sociology. To shift from the
study of social control to that of social change is not a simple
shift in research topic. The study of social change is part of a
long tradition with a philosophical framework within which not

only concepts but relations, the meaning of meaning, and the expectations for theory are all inherently related in a coherent whole. Not only did the subdiscipline of sociology, as we know it, emerge from the fragmentation of this tradition, its effect, if not purpose, has been to deny it.

In this denial, it is not only areas of social experience which have become invisible but also the organic links between this experience and our Weltanschauung (and, as here, the language to express it). So we no longer explore why we think as we do. We deal with concepts as though they can be plucked at will out of context, as though they do not entail the philosophy within which they have meaning.

It is with Hopkins that Wallerstein has collaborated for many years in the development of the world system perspective. So, in these final paired papers on theoretical and methodological issues which arise in working in this perspective, it is interesting to see how they study social change. Both deal, here, with social relations as structure and process. Both discuss, at one point, the periphery of the world system. Hopkins's approach is more analytical, Wallerstein's more historical.

Hopkins is using core-periphery relations as an example of the way, in one scientific mode of thought, the end points of relations are reified, with the relations of which they are part made conceptually invisible. We are then left with "core" and "periphery" as mere classificatory terms, neither grounded theoretically nor productive analytically. Their relations, now lost to sight, are those of the division of labor in the accumulation of capital (in which Hopkins, with Wallerstein, includes continuing "primitive accumulation"). With the end-points of this core-periphery relationship reified as world regions, the search begins, he says, for what links them. "Trade" becomes the link instead of remaining just one facet of the relationship known as the development of underdevelopment.

Wallerstein, in the part of his discussion dealing with his own work, also views structure as process. In this view, social relations of production are transformed into processes of proletarianization and of bourgeoisification (with contradictions made invisible?). In Wallerstein's (market) world system, unequal exchange extends to the sphere of circulation among his zones with their geographic class relations. In the process of bourgeoisification, the core bourgeoisie gets the greater share of the surplus value from the original bourgeois receiver. In the process of peripheralization, that is, of inclusion in the world system through its expansion, the worker undergoes proletarianization. Historically, the "part-life-time proletarian household" supports capital accumulation at less than the physiological minimum wage. It does this from noncapitalist sources: the garden plot, the gifts from relatives, and others. In becoming a complete proletarian, i.e., producing completely within the capitalist economy, the worker increases his real income and thus increases world demand. In this historically derived process of proletarianization the relation of this worker is to the accumulation process. In Hopkins's analytical derivation it is to the capitalist in the process of capital accumulation.

Core and periphery are just one dimension of one of the many issues reviewed in these concluding papers. With them, most of the problems in this academic approach to social change had emerged at the conference: whether social change can be conceived in general analytical terms or can only, or best, be analyzed in more specific historical forms; whether world capitalism is best studied as a whole or, again, through specific historical circumstances and processes within it; whether Marx's analysis of capitalism is adequate for understanding it in its present global phase and, if not, how best to modify and extend his analysis; whether Wallerstein's perspective will serve to do this and, if so, how best to develop it both analytically and historically.

One problem was not raised but emerged clearly. Working in the capitalist world economy on a socialist analysis of the demise of capitalism risks intellectual cooptation similar and related to the political subversion of progressive forces described in the papers on revolution and counterrevolution and to which Wallerstein alludes, perhaps, in the fifth part of his agenda. Sharing our awareness of this problem, as well as those more specific to our work in progress, can only "help make socialism more than a possibility."

NOTE

1. "More serious are the conceptual problems, which have not always been clearly confronted by historians—a fact which does not preclude good work (horses can be recognized and ridden by those who can't define them), but which suggests that we have been slow to face the more general problems of social structure and relations and their transformation" E.J. Hobsbawm, 1971.

REFERENCES

HOBSBAWM, E.J. (1971). "From social history to the history of society." Daedalus, 100(1):36.
SKOCPOL, T. (1977). "Wallerstein's world capitalist system: A theoretical and historical critique." American Journal of Sociology, 82(5):1075-1090.
WALLERSTEIN, I. (1974a). The modern world-system: Capitalist agriculture and the origins of the European world-economy in the sixteenth century. New York: Academic Press.
——— (1974b). "The rise and future demise of the world capitalist system: Concepts for comparative analysis." Comparative Studies in History and Society, 16(September): 387-415.
——— (1976). "Modernization: Requiescat in pace." Pp. 131-135 in L. Coser and O. Larsen (eds.), The uses of controversy in sociology. New York: Free Press.

PART 1

THE STATE AND THE WORLD SYSTEM

Chapter 1

MARXIST THEORIES OF THE STATE
IN WORLD SYSTEM ANALYSIS

Fred Block

My subject is how we theorize within the world system
perspective. The argument has three parts. I begin with the
claim that existing Marxist theories of the state place a strong
explanatory emphasis on the consciousness of dominant classes
in explaining state policy and the use of such theories in world
system analysis creates unnecessary analytic problems. In the
second part, I argue for an alternative version of the Marxist
theory of the state. In brief, the alternative version places more
emphasis on structure and relegates class intentionality to a
secondary position, which, I argue, is far more consistent with
the world system framework. Finally, I try to show how this
alternative formulation can be used concretely by reviewing the
Marxist debate on "ultra-imperialism."

There is a tendency whenever intellectual breakthroughs
occur, whenever new concepts are developed, simply to add those
new concepts onto an already existing conceptual structure. But
the danger in doing that is that the full implications of the new
concept are cut short or lost or underdeveloped because it is

Author's Note: This is a revised version of the paper that was given at the American
University conference.

forced to coexist with the established conceptual apparatus. I am arguing that this has happened with the development and elaboration of the world system perspective. That new perspective has simply been added onto a lot of our existing intellectual baggage, particularly existing theories in Marxism about the relationship between capitalist classes and the state.

This fusion has created some intellectual problems. To start with, Marxist theories of the state, especially those used within world system analyses, place a strong emphasis on the consciousness of the capitalist class, or at least sectors of that class, in determining state policies. Even when writers talk about the relative autonomy of the state, it is still assumed that at some level of analysis, one can talk about the interests or intentions of some sectors of the dominant class being reflected in state policy. In short, even in the more subtle Marxist analyses, it is assumed that some sector of the capitalist class has a fully developed strategic conception of what the state should do both in the international arena and domestically, and that conception is a key input into state policymaking.

This mode of analysis with its emphasis on consciousness and intentionality of class actors clashes with the world system perspective, which, as I read it, is primarily a structural argument. The core of the world system perspective is the idea that standard social science and historiography have been fixated on the level of appearances. When one looks simply at the level of appearances, one sees different nation states and different regions, each with its own unique history, evolving according to its own internal dynamics. In contrast, the world system perspective insists that behind the level of appearances, there is a structured reality, there is a capitalist world system with its divisions among core, periphery, and semi-periphery. That structural reality of the capitalist world system determines a great deal of what goes on in the seemingly independent nation states or regions. The structural thrust of the argument is clearest when Wallerstein (1974a) talks about developments in the Soviet Union and China. In essence, he argues that in spite of what Soviet theoreticians and state managers might have thought, the fundamental reality was that socialist construction was taking place within a capitalist world system and that fundamentally distorted or limited what the Soviets, and the Chinese, are capable of doing. That is a very powerful structural argument because regardless of anyone's intentions, the real forces are the structural relations of a capitalist world system that unfold behind the backs of social actors.

When one combines the world system perspective's structural emphasis with Marxist theories of the state's emphasis on class intentionality, the result is not a dialectical synthesis, but analytic confusion. The two theories just do not fit together properly. The analytic confusion is subtle, but I can give some examples from Wallerstein's (1974b) book that, I think, make the point. There is a strange kind of asymmetry to Wallerstein's argument about the rise and fall of core nations. When the rise of a core nation is discussed, the explanation for the rise often draws heavily on the intentionality of class actors, whereas when a nation's decline is being accounted for, the explanations tend to be structural. For example, nations decline because there is an inflationary process that develops that makes the economy uncompetitive or because there is an overinvestment in the political costs of empire that happens inadvertently. In short, nations rise as a result of class intentionality and decline because of factors that emerge behind the back of social actors. This raises the critical question: "If they were so smart then, what happened to them later?" Obviously there are ways of answering the question, such as arguing that it is easy to be smart when structural forces are working with you, but as the argument stands, the asymmetry is problematic.

Another problem that Wallerstein slips into results from the fact that within the existing Marxist theories of the state, it is natural to talk about capitalists within a nation state having a developed class consciousness. This class consciousness includes a strategic sense; capitalists, or sectors of the class, know what has to be done to maintain their rule. So when one combines the Marxist theory of the state with the world system perspective, it is only natural to extend that capitalist class consciousness internationally. Hence, Wallerstein suggests at a number of points that capitalist classes within nations have a developed sense of international strategy and this consciousness is reflected in the policies of core states. Now it is already difficult to make a convincing empirical case that capitalist classes have that kind of strategic consciousness in terms of policies within nation states. But when one adds that further level—that capitalists have some kind of international strategic consciousness—I think one runs into real problems of evidence and explanation. Of course, one can always find a few members of a ruling class who possess far-sighted views of what has to be done by the state both domestically and internationally, but to argue that such individuals are some kind of direct representatives of their class seems quite problematic to me.

These criticisms should become clearer as I state the alternative formulations that I think make it possible to avoid some of these analytic confusions. The alternative is a Marxist theory of the state that is primarily structural, relegating capitalist class consciousness to a secondary role. I have developed this argument more fully elsewhere (Block, 1977); what I will try to do here is provide an abbreviated version of the argument. This will obviously be incomplete, raising as many questions as it answers, but my purpose is only to give a sense of the direction in which the alternative line of argument would proceed.

This structural view of the capitalist state does not start with the idea of the relative autonomy of the state because that formulation continues to impute high levels of consciousness to the capitalist class. I want to begin with the idea of a sharp division of labor between those who devote themselves to accumulation and those who devote themselves to managing the state apparatus. I want to argue that the division of labor creates differences of interests—state managers are interested in expanding their own power within the structural situation in which they find themselves—and differences in world views. The ideologies of state managers and capitalists are going to be different because of their different structural locations. The critical point that separates this argument from the liberalism that some people will charge me with is that this division of labor occurs within a structural framework. The structural framework is the reason that, despite the division of interests between capitalists and state managers, the general tendency is for state managers to act in the general interests of capital. Hence, the key to the argument is the analysis of the structural framework.

The two aspects of the structural framework that I want to emphasize are the idea of business confidence and the ways in which demands of subordinate classes are processed. In a capitalist economy, the rate of investment is dependent upon entrepreneurial or managerial decisions and those decisions are made partly in response to simple economic variables. But there is also a more intangible element to investment decisions—the businessperson's perception of how promising is the general political-economic environment. When these perceptions are aggregated across the whole economy, they can be termed the level of business confidence. When business confidence is in decline or threatening to decline (and there was a recent illustration of this in the period between the election and the beginning of the Carter administration when business confidence was threatening to decline, unless Carter made various concessions, such as appointing conservative business types to key posts in the administration), state managers are in trouble. Regardless of their ideology, state managers are dependent upon maintaining adequate levels of business confidence for a series of different reasons. For one thing, the level of business confidence will determine the rate of investment and that will determine the rate of employment. The more unemployment there is, the less political support the regime is likely to have, in general. So in order to protect themselves from political dissatisfaction, state managers want to keep business confidence up. Business confidence is also important because the rate of investment determines the flow of revenues to the state itself. The amount of freedom that state managers have in a competitive nation state system to spend money on armaments is also then a function of the rate of business investment and the level of business confidence. Finally, the level of business confidence has other international ramifications. In a capitalist world economy where trade can move capital across national boundaries in response to market forces, a domestic decline of business confidence will usually generate a decline in international business confidence. International bankers are then reluctant to lend to that nation, and other businesspeople act to disinvest, so the consequence is an international payments crisis. Such a crisis presents state managers with a whole set of difficult problems that they would sooner avoid by acting in the first place to halt the decline in business confidence.

In short, for all these reasons, state managers are generally constrained from doing things that would damage business confidence and they have a strong incentive to use what power they have to improve business confidence, that is, improve the investment climate. The point I want to stress is that business confidence is not like a capitalist class consciousness. On the contrary, business confidence is based on a very short-term, short-sighted perception of the environment. A capitalist class consciousness implies a long-range, strategic point of view. The clearest way of thinking of this difference is the example of FDR during the Great Depression. Roosevelt was continually saying to the business community that he was acting in their general class interest; he was trying to save capitalism. But business confidence remained at low levels; businesspeople were far less impressed by FDR's pleas than they were by such troubling signs as the rise of industrial unionism.

The other key aspect of the structural framework is the way in which demands by subordinate classes (working class, petite bourgeoisie, and peasants) are processed by state managers. It has been demands by such subordinate classes that have played a key role in expanding the state's role in the delivery of services and in the regulation of markets. Faced with demands from below, state managers attempt to avert political turmoil or electoral defeat by pushing outward the boundaries of state action, even against the resistance of business confidence. But even though the pressure to expand the state's role often comes from below, the dynamic is different once the expansion has occurred. Then, state managers have reasons to use their expanded powers to improve the investment climate, that is, in ways that are in the general interests of capital. For example, pressures from below are important in extending educational opportunities in capitalist societies, but once an expanded educational system is created, state managers will orient the educational system toward the creation of the kind of labor force that capital needs. They will do so because they have an interest in improving the investment climate.

Together, these two aspects of the structural framework provide a model in which the rationality of the capitalist state, or its capacity to act in the general interests of capital, cannot be reduced to the consciousness of a sector of capital or the consciousness of state managers themselves. The argument is that the rationality of the capitalist state emerges out of the three-sided relationship between state managers, capital, and subordinate classes. The rationality emerges largely behind the backs of the social actors involved.

The virtue of this model is that it allows one to get away from the standard Marxist methodological tool of assuming that state policies always reflect the intentionality of a social class or sector of a class. It renders obsolete the procedure of looking for a specific social base for any particular state policy. Of course, there are always capitalist special interests attempting to get the state to act in their favor, as, for example, the oil companies lobbying for energy policies that would maximize their profits. But when we are talking about the strategic level, the kind of state policies that rise above specific industrial interests because they are oriented to maintaining the conditions necessary for continued class rule domestically and keeping open possibilities for economic expansion abroad, then such reductionism is unnecessary. The distinction between "objective" and "subjective" is useful here. One can say that a policy objectively benefited a particular social class, but that is very different from saying that that social class, or sector of a class, subjectively wanted that policy, or that its intentions were a critical element in policy development.

A historical illustration should clarify what is at stake in this argument. One of the recurring issues in Marxist discussions of the world capitalist system is the consequences of growing economic interpenetration among the core capitalist powers. Writers from Kautsky (1970) to the present have argued that the internationalization of investment is creating a kind of "ultra-imperialism" in which the interlocking of interests among a small number of giant capitalists in the core nations will create a new international ruling class. The common interests of this international ruling class will then preclude serious conflict among the nations of the core. Not only will interimperialist war become unthinkable, but the core nations will present an increasingly united front toward the nations of the periphery and semi-periphery.

The standard critique of this position derives from Lenin (1939:117-121). It goes as follows: while a system of ultra-imperialism might be stable temporarily, it is bound to happen, because of uneven development, that economic groups in a particular capitalist nation will become dissatisfied with the prevailing arrangments for sharing the global surplus. These groups will push their state to demand a renegotiation of the existing "rules of the game" on the grounds that their share is no longer commensurate with their increased size and financial power. However, these attempts at revision are likely to be resisted by other nations, and the result would probably be a breakdown of the ultra-imperialist order. Those economic interests that feel they are being cheated will use their respective states to act in an increasingly aggressive way toward the anti-revisionist powers, resulting in trade wars and possibly open interimperialist conflict.

This line of argument, however, seems to become less compelling as the process of economic interpenetration progresses further and further. If some two or three hundred multinational corporations dominate the world economy, and most of these corporations are active in all of the core nations and are closely intertwined with each other in a variety of different arrangements, then it becomes harder to imagine a particular nationally based set of economic interests being aggrieved enough and powerful enough to disrupt the fabric of interimperialist cooperation. On the contrary, one would imagine that such a system would be quite flexible in its capacity to coopt new corporate groups, for example, those that develop in semi-peripheral areas into an elaborate system of interlocking corporate power.

There is, however, another line of criticism of the ultra-imperialism argument, but it requires examining the theory of the state implicit in that position. The ultra-imperialism argument assumes that state policies wil generally reflect the intentionality of the dominant capitalists. Once these dominant capitalists recognize that economic interpenetration among core nations has made interimperialist conflict not only unnecessary but positively harmful, they will exert their influence to see that state managers act accordingly. And the results of that influence would be a continuation of interimperialist cooperation.

But what if state policies do not always reflect the intentionality of dominant capitalists? Then it might be the case that even though the dominant capitalists want to preserve interimperialist cooperation, state managers find they have little alternative but to intensify interimperialist conflict. If this were the case, then no matter how far the development of an international ruling class had progressed, ultra-imperialism would still be unstable, and interimperialist conflict might resume.

The argument I have made about the division of labor between state managers and capitalists provides an explanation of how the interests of capitalists and state managers might diverge, but what specific circumstances could lead to such sharp divergences on such a critical issue as the maintenance of interimperialist cooperation? If state managers perceived that the existing rules of the game of the ultra-imperialist system were creating such havoc in their domestic political economy that extremist movements of the left or of the right were threatening their control of state power, then those state managers would very likely begin agitating for a revision of these rules. Their dominant capitalists might well be prospering as a result of global operations, but if high levels of domestic unemployment or inflation or other economic dislocations were creating political turmoil, the state managers might well ignore the pleadings of those capitalists and use their power to disrupt the fabric of interimperialist cooperation. In short, the argument is similar to Lenin's, but it is the state managers who push for a renegotiation of the international arrangements.

As long as one assumes that state policy will reflect the intentionality of the dominant capitalists, the ultra-imperialism argument seems unassailable. But once one adopts a more sophisticated model which recognizes that the intentionality of capitalists is only one part of the structural matrix that shapes the response of state managers operating in a capitalist world system, then the weaknesses of the ultra-imperialism position become apparent. Since a capitalist world economy will always be characterized by combined and uneven development, the process of economic integration among capitals is bound to create severe economic strains in some of the nations of the core. If those economic strains provoke a serious political response, then state managers will be under strong pressure to improve the terms of their nation's integration into the world system. The inevitability of such attempts makes it difficult to conceive of a stable, long-term system of ultra-imperialism.

This argument also makes it possible to resolve a contradiction that has bothered me for a while. Karl Polanyi, whose work was a critical building block in our understanding of the capitalist world system, argued in *The Great Transformation* (1957:9-19) that *haute finance*, the major banking houses, played a key role in preserving the peace during the second half of the century between Waterloo and Sarajevo. According to Polanyi, the great financial families, with their offices in every major European capital, did not want a general European war to break out. Whenever a crisis occurred, the financial interests would use their considerable influence with the heads of state, who were literally indebted to them, to urge them to draw back from the brink of war. But Lenin argued that Finance Capital (which would seem to overlap considerably with haute finance) was responsible for the outbreak of World War I. The two apparently conflicting positions can be reconciled with the distinction between intentionality and structure. Haute finance wanted peace and presumably was an unsuccessful peace interest in the last hours before World War I. It was unsuccessful, however, because the development of the whole structure of finance capitalism had created objective conditions within which state managers felt they had little alternative but to go to war. In sum, one might say that the road to war is paved with peaceful intentions, and the road to analytic confusion in Marxism is paved with an exaggerated concern with class intentionality.

REFERENCES

BLOCK, F. (1977). "The ruling class does not rule." Socialist Revolution, 33(May-June): 6-28.

KAUTSKY, K. (1970). "Ultra-imperialism." New Left Review, 59(January-Feburary): 41-46.

LENIN, V.I. (1939). Imperialism: The highest stage of capitalism. New York: International.

POLANYI, K. (1957). The great transformation. Boston: Beacon.

WALLERSTEIN, I. (1974a). "The rise and future demise of the world capitalist system." Comparative Studies in Society and History, 16(September):387-415.

——— (1974b). The modern world-system: Capitalist agriculture and the origins of the European world economy in the sixteenth century. New York: Academic.

Chapter 2

POLITICAL TRANSFORMATION IN GERMANY
AND THE UNITED STATES

Richard Rubinson

This paper analyses the political conditions which affect the development of states by focusing on crucial aspects of that process in Germany and the United States in the middle of the 19th century. This study of these two well-known cases is motivated not by the appearance of new data, but rather by the necessity to understand these instances of development from the theoretical perspective of world-systems analysis. Most analyses of these countries tend to emphasize factors specific to each of them without attention to the similarity and inter-dependence of the German and United States processes of development. The specific problem addressed is to understand the conditions which allow countries to move into the core of the capitalist world-system.

The crucial role of state action and organization for national economic development is well known. Studies have shown that the formation of a political elite committed to the goal of national economic development is necessary for such development (Black et al., 1975; Skocpol, 1976; Trimberger, 1972). These studies have concluded that the most important factors determining the emergence of such a ruling stratum are the relationships between the state and the major class interests in the country. But of equal importance for national development is the existence of the *possibility* for development when such a political stratum is in power. The history of the world capitalist system is marked by numerous instances of ruling groups committed to major economic transformation either being displaced from power or altering their policies because the possibility for national development did not exist. The most important factors determining the possibility for national economic transformation are a function of what is occurring in the world-system and the relationship of the country to the system (Wallerstein, 1974).

The reason why these two sets of factors are so crucial derives from three structural characteristics of countries attempting to develop within the world-system. First, since such countries are already part of the world division of labor, certain dominant or crucial economic producers are involved in a set of complementary relationships with producers in core areas. The advantages accruing to these producers tend to direct their political aims toward maintaining the present position of the country in the world division of labor. Second, prior development of the world-system will have placed producers of commodities which compete directly with those of core areas at a relative competitive disadvantage in the world market as a whole and often within their own national economy. For these groups of national producers, their economic interests lie in breaking away from the dominance of core countries in order to shift their country's position in the world division of labor. Their political aims, then, lead to policies which directly oppose those groups of producers which are involved in complementary relationships with producers in core countries. Third, these divergent political tendencies between these different groups of producers tend to weaken the ability of the state either to direct a concerted effort of major economic transformation or to carry out the aggressive political action vis-à-vis core countries which is necessary for development.

Given such conditions, the initial problem of national development is fundamentally a political problem of reorganizing the relationships among the state and the different groups of producers. But such a fundamental political transformation is exceedingly difficult because of the way economic interests operate in the world capitalist system. For the goal of economic producers is not national development, but profit. Significant national development is likely to occur only when the possibilities for profit among the range of national producers coincides. For then the concerted and aggressive state action necessary for development receives the support of all the major national economic producers. But since national development is fundamentally a *shift in the position* of a country in the world division of labor and not merely an increase in the absolute size of national product, the development of any one country will cause a relative disadvantage for producers in core areas. Such a shift will create political resistance from these groups, and they will attempt to use their own national state apparatus and superior competitive advantage to maintain their position and prevent change. Consequently, events in the world-system must be favorable to allow for the possibility of national development. National development, then, requires a political transformation of class relationships both within the country and within the world division of labor, along with occurrences in the system as a whole which allow for the possibility of development.

This paper analyzes this political transformation in Germany and the United States. In 1850 Britain was the hegemonic power in the world. By the turn of the century, both Germany and the United States had successfully challenged Britain's supremacy to become the dominant core countries in the world. Between 1840 and 1880 both countries experienced a fundamental political transformation. In Germany this transformation occurred during the era of Bismarck's Unification; in the United States during the era of the Civil War and Reconstruction. What occurred in each case was a three part political change. First, industrial producers, which were directly competing with producers in England and other core areas, came to have their interests institutionalized within the state. Second, certain economic producers, whose interests were previously opposed, came to have political interests which converged. And third, the economies of both Germany and the United States became nationally integrated. It was thus a three part political transformation which occurred in Germany and the United States which set the political conditions for their economic transformations into core areas of the world-system.

THE WORLD ECONOMY IN THE MID-19th CENTURY: POSSIBILITIES FOR TRANSFORMATION

The decade of the 1860s was a period of political transformation and upheaval. Most striking was that the United States, Germany, and Japan, three of the countries which were to become new core powers, each experienced their major political transformations at this time. The United States Civil War occurred from 1861 to 1865; German Unification occurred between 1862 and 1867; and the Meiji restoration in Japan occurred in 1868. During this same period, Italy was politically unified and the Habsburg Empire was reorganized. There was also significant political upheavals in Turkey in 1866, in Poland in 1863, in China in 1862, and in Peru in 1865, to indicate some others. Clearly this was a time of significant political reorganization for many areas throughout the world.

The political transformations in Germany, the United States, and Japan have been studied extensively by many analysts, most notably by Barrington Moore (1966). But in his analysis, each case was studied independently; and he had no theoretical framework to provide any reason for supposing that the close timing of these transformations was more than coincidental. But these events were not coincidental but a consequence of what was happening in the world-system as a whole. Moore's neglect of this phenomenon was mainly due to his purpose of analyzing these political transformations as causes of different forms of regime. But whatever the variations in the German, United States, and Japanese regimes, these transformations were similar in that they set the political conditions for those countries to become strong core states. To understand these transformations, we must begin with an analysis of what was happening in the world-system and begin by asking why new core states *could* arise in this period.

The 19th century was a period of tremendous geographic expansion in the world-economy. From 1800 to 1870, the European world-economy became a truly global economy. This was also the period of the second industrial revolution, marked most clearly by the shift from textiles to capital goods industries based on coal and iron and railroads. And from 1820, industrialization began to spread throughout Europe and North America.

This geographic expansion was a function of many factors, including technological improvements in shipping and military armaments (Woodruff, 1973). But economic conditions in Britain, the hegemonic core power, seem crucial. For Britain's prior economic success had created vast surpluses of investment capital, far outstripping the opportunities for profitable investment within England. As Eric Hobsbawm (1968:112) says, "there were vast accumulations of capital burning holes in their owners' pockets." Much of that capital was invested abroad, mostly in the financing of the world's railroads and in the expansion of cash-crop agriculture. This vast capital flow, then, became one of the forces leading to the geographic expansion of the 19th century.

Britain's industrial success also led to the spread of industrialization, primarily throughout Europe and North America. As Britain shifted from textiles to capital goods, textile manufacturing in other areas such as Germany and Italy prospered. Her competitive advantage in industrial products shifted her foreign policy to one of free trade; and after 1820 Britain allowed the export of machines, industrial blueprints, and skilled workers which spread the technology of industrialization throughout Europe and North America (Fielden, 1969; Henderson, 1965). Much of Britain's surplus capital was also invested in industrial production in Europe and North America. This increasing industrialization created large demands for food and new raw materials, which in turn led to the geographic expansion of the world-economy.

The details of this expansion are well known and need not be recounted. The enormous scope of this expansion is captured by such descriptions of the period as in Hobsbawm's "global economy" and in Woodruff's "creation of an international economy." Much of Asia, Africa, and remaining areas of Latin America became incorporated as peripheral areas. Before the 1840s, the size and scale of international economic operations were relatively modest. From 1800 to 1830, total international trade increased 30%; but from 1840 to 1870, it increased 500%. And after 1850 economic crises had become worldwide in scope and timing (Hobsbawm, 1968:139; 1975; Woodruff, 1973).

The result of this expansion was an absolute increase in the size of the capitalist world-system, brought about by the increase in the size of the peripheral areas of the system. The fact that in the 1860s the United States, Germany, and Japan began their organization as core areas must be traced to this expansion. For the creation of these three core areas meant an increase in the absolute size of the core, which was made possible by the increase in the size of the peripheral areas of the system.

The possibilities for some countries or areas to shift positions in the world division of labor is most often created by weakness in the core areas of the system. Thus, world economic contraction and increased political or economic conflict among core states allows the opportunity for some semi-peripheral and peripheral areas to alter their positions. But this advance by some areas occurs at the expense of others, reflecting the zero-sum character of much national development within the world-system. But a second possibility arises when there is an increase in the absolute size of the system itself. For as new areas are peripheralized, some areas can seize the opportunity to politically and economically reorganize. The creation of core areas in the United States, Germany, and Japan meant an absolute increase in the size of the core; not merely a zero-sum shift in which their transformations were matched by the decline of some other core powers into semi-peripheral status. This increase was made possible by the increase in the size of the periphery.

The expansion of the size of the peripheral areas of the system allows for the expansion of the size of core areas for two basic reasons. First, increased peripheralization means an increase in the amount of labor in the system, and this increase allows more areas to capture a larger share of the value produced by this increase of labor. Second, with such an increase, more areas can shift their position in the division of labor to specialize in core activities and benefit from the structure of unequal exchange between core and periphery.

This increase in the size of the core, then, allows for the *possibility* that some states can politically and economically reorganize themselves into core areas. In the 1860s, the United States, Germany, and Japan were able to take advantage of the increase in peripheralization to transform themselves into core areas. It is important to note, however, that, even though the size of the core increased, the success of some countries in this case also meant the failure of others to become core powers. The success of the United States and Germany, for example, meant that Italy and Austria were to remain semi-peripheral areas. The political upheavals of the 1860s, then, represent in large part the response of areas in the world to the new possibilities created by the expansion of the world-economy.

If the expansion of the world economy in the 19th century created the possibility for some areas to become core powers, the next question becomes: What is the nature of the process by which some countries succeeded and other countries failed? We now turn to an examination of this process in Germany and the United States, two of the areas that succeeded in this competition.

POLITICAL TRANSFORMATION IN GERMANY

GERMANY IN THE WORLD ECONOMY, 1840-1860

In the 1830s the area that became modern Germany was among the most backward areas in Europe. The area was the most rural; its farms and industrial establishments were among the smallest; its guild system the strongest; the area economically unintegrated; and its financial and legal system the most anti-quated. Dominated by the aristocratic landed classes of Prussia and politically fragmented, the area appeared to most observers as the last area in Europe likely to industrialize. It consisted of basically three distinctive economic areas occupying very different roles in the world-economy (Borchardt, 1973; Clapham, 1966; Hammerow, 1966; Henderson, 1961; and Hoffmann, 1963).

The eastern area of Prussia consisted of Junker estates producing grain and timber for both internal and external consumption. Prussian grain production was increasing, due to both increases in productivity and increases in arable land. From 1840 to 1860, Prussia combined both self-sufficiency in food supply with a considerable export market in grain, with the bulk of grain exports going to Britain. Although exports were good (the price of grain remained below British prices until the 1850s), the Junkers still faced relative decline, especially among the smaller estate holders, the Junker squirearchy. Junker money, in a typical fashion, went into the pockets of financiers through debt and credit arrangements. From 1835 to 1864, there was a 200% turnover in ownership of some 12,000 large estates, 14,400 sales of estates, and 1,300 fore-closures. So even though grain production and sales were good, the Junkers as a class were suffering a relative decline in their economic position due to financial difficulties, a decline which became even greater after 1850 as the terms of trade came to favor industrial over agrarian commodities.[1] As grain exporters, the political interests of the Junkers lay in the direction of free trade because of their heavy dependence on the world market, since in the 19th century, as now, the world market created the demand for grain and other food. The Junkers also had no interest in German unification and integration, since a politically and economically fragmented Germany assured the dominance of Prussia within the area. The Junkers were politically dominant, since the Prussian state was the major political organization in central Europe, and the Junkers dom-inated this state through their control of the civil and military bureaucracies. The financial problems only served to increase the tie between the Prussian state and the Junker interests, since indebtedness and foreclosures tended to drive the less fortunate Junkers into the state bureaucracy.[2]

The northern German states were dominated by merchant and financial interests. The trade and shipping interests of these areas were, in turn, dominated by British interests; so much so that in the 1840s Hamburg was known as "the commission agent of England." Throughout the 1840s, England cultivated its ties with the northern states, and, in 1844 to 1846, these states signed a series of free-trade treaties with England to prevent their full participation in the German Customs Union, the Zollverein. Free-trade treaties were also signed with the United States for the cotton trade. Financial and credit institutions in Germany were weak, and banks catered to the financial requirements of both German and foreign governments and the aristocracy, but not to industry. The political interests of these states, then, lay in free trade and the maintenance of secure commercial and financial ties with England (Hammerow, 1966,1969; and Taylor, 1962).

The west and south were the primary industrial areas of Germany. German industrialization started in weaving and mining, with the major centers in Saxony and the Rhineland. But industrialization in Germany had to contend with a complicated series of internal tariffs, taxes, political rules, and guild privileges which dotted the politically fragmented region and restricted the size and integration of the domestic market. Nevertheless, the pace of industrialization quickened in the 1840s in Germany, as it tended to do throughout Europe and North America. The volume of goods moving along the Rhine doubled from 1836 to 1846; there was significant factory expansion; a growing German textile manufacture exporting to Poland and Austria; and a spurt of railway construction (Borchardt, 1973). Throughout the 1840s and 1850s the economic position of the industrial interests within Germany tended to grow stronger relative to the Junkers. This situation was helped by the fact that the terms of trade after 1850 shifted to the advantage of industrial over agrarian goods.

But German industry was still very weak relative to England and other countries. For example, in 1849 German cotton weavers bought 62% of their yarn from abroad. British capital goods were especially important in the establishment of German industry. The first railroads were equipped largely with British engines, cars, and rails; and they were built largely with British capital. French, British, Belgian, and Swiss enterprises were prominent in Germany; and most of the foreign investment in the area was in industry. Machinery almost always was imported from Britain or the United States. The weak international position of German industrialization was reflected in foreign trade. The rate of growth of international trade tended to decline up to 1850. Clapham estimates that between 1840 and 1850 imports per capita increased but exports decreased. German integration in international trade fell further behind that of Britain, France, and the United States. Exports consisted largely of unprocessed foodstuffs and agricultural produce. Fully manufactured goods accounted for only 18% of exports, and the crisis in the linen industry due to British competition tended to lower this percentage even more.[3]

Throughout the 1840s and 1850s, then, German industrialization was increasing, but it was localized, not competitive on the world market, and heavily dependent upon and interpenetrated by foreign capital. Domestic manufacturers were constantly threatened by foreign competition. It was the weak international position of the industrialists that moved their political interests in the direction of tariffs and other forms of political protection for the domestic market. German unification became another major political goal, since unification was necessary to rid the area of internal barriers to trade and to enlarge the size of the domestic market. With these political aims, the industrialists became the natural allies of the liberals' political program of nationalism and liberalism: nationalism because that meant political and economic unification, and liberalism because that meant one way to reduce the political power of the Junkers (Hammerow, 1966; Taylor, 1962). The economic position of the industrialists in the world-economy, then, moved them into a political position which was almost exactly opposite to that of the Junkers and commercial classes, whose interests lay in the direction of free trade, maintenance of their complementary ties with Britain, and political fragmentation of central Europe (Hammerow, 1966; Taylor, 1962).

These opposing economic and political interests of the industrialists and the Junkers clashed in the Revolution of 1848. For a major part of that revolution was the attempt by the liberals and industrialists to gain political power within Germany at the expense of the king and the Junkers. Their slogans were liberalism and nationalism; and, in the context of 1848, both of these meant greater political power for the industrialists, the unification of Germany, and economic nationalism and protection.

Although the initial success of the Revolution of 1848 soon fell to the Prussian reaction, the industrial interests did gain in several significant ways. First, they demonstrated their increased political importance as a threat to Junker dominance, a threat that became a major goal of Bismarck's policy to neutralize. Institutionally, the rising political power of the industrialists was symbolized by the Prussian parliament, consisting largely of lawyers, civil servants, and other liberals. Second, the industrial interests gained several important economic benefits: an increased role for the state in industrial development, the elimination of many customs barriers and internal impediments to trade, and some general tariff protection. Thus, although the major political aims of the industrialists did not succeed, one outcome of 1848 was that the economic interests and policies of that class began to be institutionalized within the state (Fischer, 1963; Hammerow, 1966; Taylor, 1962).

The decade of the 1850s only served to increase their economic power even further, for this was a decade of extreme industrial prosperity. Pig iron production grew rapidly; the production of capital and consumer goods more than doubled; and the volume of foreign trade doubled. In what would be the beginning of a pattern, the industrial interests had failed to gain direct political power, but traded this goal for economic prosperity.

POLITICAL TRANSFORMATION, 1860-1880

The economic and political situation in Germany in 1860 was typical of much of Europe and North America at the time. The landed classes were politically dominant, but their previous economic supremacy was being challenged by increasing industrial production. And the different economic roles these groups occupied in the world-economy operated to put them into political opposition to one another. But from 1860 to 1880, Germany's political transformation was to set the conditions for it to outstrip every other area in Europe and to enter the core of the world-system.

There were three aspects to this transformation. First, the economic interests and policies of the industrial and manufacturing groups became institutionalized within the German state. Second, the German economy became nationalized and integrated through the creation of a single domestic market and protection of crucial areas of the market from foreign competition. And third, the crucial economic producers, the Junkers and the industrialists, came to have certain similar interests which allowed them to form a political-economic coalition which dominated the state. This convergence of interests between classes that had been previously opposed seems to be the crucial reason why Germany was able to outstrip other European countries and become part of the core of the world-system. For the pattern in the world-system is that where the dominant economic producers in an area have divergent interests, the state remains weak and unable to solve the political problem of development. This is the typical situation in peripheral areas. Where the range of crucial economic producers comes to have convergent political interests, the coalition formed among them strengthens the state and allows it to solve the political problem of development. This is the case in the core areas of the world-system.

The significance of Bismarck's unification was that it had the consequence of creating these conditions. Bismarck's unification from 1861 to 1865 started this process of convergence, of forming industrial and agrarian interests into a working coalition. At first this coalition was politically imposed by Bismarck on both Junkers and industrialists, but from 1865 to 1870 changes in the world economy were to make this initial coalition into a solid political-economic alliance.

Bismarck was able to unify Germany by bringing the opposing interests of Junkers and industrialists together in a compromise that was initially minimally acceptable to both. The Junkers grudgingly accepted it because it insured their political dominance within a united Germany; while the industrialists accepted Prussian rule because it gave them economic prosperity by establishing many elements of their economic goals. The peasants and urban working class, having previously learned that neither Junker nor liberal were their allies, went along under the inducement of social security and the vote (Hammerow, 1966; Taylor, 1962).

Accounts of Bismarck's political skills in forming this coalition abound. But what must be explained is why he had the freedom to maneuver to create such a coalition between opposing interests. The answer to this lies in the relative economic strength of Junker and industrialist by 1860. For by 1860, the industrial and agrarian classes were relatively equal in power. Industrial strength had been growing while Junker economic strength had shown a relative decline, though the overall position of the Junkers was strengthened through their control of the state. Thus both groups were relatively equal in power, with neither able to dominate the other. The continual struggle between the two had made for the politics of the 1850s. Under such a condition, the state is able to attain a degree of autonomy and maneuverability that it does not often have. Hence, the vectors of economic interest provided the condition for relative autonomous political maneuvering by Bismarck. Added to this major condition were two other factors. The years immediately prior to unification were periods of relative expansion for both industrial and agrarian classes. The German iron industry had taken great leaps forward and industrial production was increasing in general. Also, agriculture thrived during mid-century and did not start its decline until after 1865. Thus, both groups were doing well in the short run and neither had any immediate economic reason to resist the larger structural situation. If one or the other had been doing poorly, they might have feared the risk of unification enough to present enough resistance to prevent Bismarck's plan. Added to this was the military problem. The military force of Prussia was controlled by the Junker-dominated military bureaucracy and it required industrial goods. Though their direct economic interest opposed unification, the foreign political threat to Prussian dominance pushed the Junkers toward coalition with the industrialists (Taylor, 1962). Thus, Bismarck's political success was a function of the fact that the worldwide economic trends of the 1850s had increased the economic position of the industrialists and weakened the economic position of the Junkers, creating a situation in the early 1860s of relative balance of the two forces within Germany. This gave him the opportunity and freedom to maneuver.

In unification, the liberals and industrialists achieved most of their important economic goals: a unified Germany which created a large internal market free of internal tariffs and cross-cutting political rules; the entrance of the state into industrial financing and internal improvements; freedom of enterprise and the destruction of guild privileges; and secular education. The Junkers maintained political control through the dominance of Prussia within united Germany, which enabled them politically to protect their economic position which was being undercut in the world market. Hence, the industrialists traded political position for economic prosperity, and the Junkers traded concessions to the industrialists for political control of the German state. Thus, German Unification institutionalized within the state the economic interests of the industrial and manufacturing classes, and it also created the economic integration of the domestic market that was necessary for industrial expansion.

German unification brought together interests which were normally opposed into a working political coalition. Such a coalition is not easy to maintain for long periods, for the political expediencies will tend to give way if they are not soon supported by mutual economic interests. But from 1865 to 1880, changes in the world-economy and Germany's position in it served to create the conditions which added economic benefit to the original political coalition. For after 1865 Prussian grain exports began to decline. The railway of Russia, and, most importantly, of the United States, brought foreign grain to Europe. After 1865 Prussian grain was slowly pushed off the world market, as the U.S. captured the grain trade with England and other European countries and even threatened to enter the German home market at the expense of the Junkers. In order to maintain their economic position, the Junkers were forced into a policy of economic protection and political supports for grain. This worked in two ways. One, a policy of tariff protection to protect the home market; and two, a policy of grain subsidies to allow Prussian grain to compete abroad. The result was the political shoring up of the Junker economic position (at the expense of the German masses who had to pay exorbitant prices for bread).[4] This shift to agricultural protection allied the economic interests of the Junkers with the industrialists, who had always been for protection. The need for industrial protection became even more acute in the 1870s, as British iron and steel began to force the German iron and steel industry out of the German market (Gerschenkron, 1943; Moore, 1966; Taylor, 1962). This marriage of iron and rye became economically cemented with the Great Tariff of 1879, in which both interests combined around protection. Changes in the world-economy had served to weaken German agriculture and drive it into an economic and political coalition with German industry, creating the political coalition which was to dominate Germany during its crucial period of development into a core power.

With the formation of this coalition, the German state was strengthened as the major economic producers came to support the aggressive political action that makes the development of an area into a core power possible: state financing of industrial production, protection of the home market for national producers, aggressive economic foreign policy to secure raw materials and outlets for exports, internal domestic policies to maintain wage rates at appropriate levels, and political support for the processes of monopolization and centralization of capital. Political convergence among the range of dominant economic producers is necessary for these policies, because without such support the opposition provided by certain producing classes will tend to undermine these political policies. It is through this process, then, that coalition among the major economic producers solves the political problem of development.

There is a tendency in historical interpretation to see the economic significance of such transformations as German Unification merely in the fact that they placed industrial interests into a position of economic power and dominance and that they destroyed the agrarian classes. But the success of German development was not just a function of industrial economic dominance, but of political coalition between the industrial and agrarian classes. Thus, the interests of both the industrialists and the Junkers were protected and built into the structure of the state. For if the agrarian interests are destroyed, then the area is placed at the dependence of the world-market and foreign competitors for its food supply. But the process of convergence in Germany allowed it to maintain relative self-sufficiency in food, a condition which is necessary for a country employing the classic mechanisms of mercantilist protection to develop. It is only when industrial and agrarian interests form such a coalition, then, that such a political path to development is able to succeed.

POLITICAL TRANSFORMATION
IN THE UNITED STATES

THE UNITED STATES IN THE WORLD-ECONOMY, 1840-1860

In the period 1840-1860, the United States, like Germany, consisted of very distinct regional economic areas. And its economic and political structure was in many ways much like Germany's. In the South, the major economic activity was cotton production, controlled by the aristocratic slave-owning class similar to the Prussian Junkers. While much of the cotton crop went north to New England textile mills, the South was heavily dependent on exports, primarily to Britain. Up to 1860, in fact, all of Britain's cotton came from the United States. This was because U.S. cotton was technically the best cotton in the world and its price declined over this time due to decline in transportation costs and increases in productivity (Fogel and Engerman, 1974; North, 1961; Potter, 1960; Woodruff, 1975).

From 1840 to 1860, cotton production expanded, but like the Prussian Junkers, much of the profits from the cotton trade ended up in the hands of the financial and commercial classes. The United States cotton trade was controlled from New York City for both financing and marketing, which in turn was controlled from England. It was English capital, in fact, which financed much of the expansion of cotton production in the U.S. between 1840-1869. The South used its cotton profits to buy manufactures from the North or from England, and food from the U.S. West. Its political interests, much like the Junkers, rested with free trade in order to find its foreign markets for cotton and to be able to buy its manufactures cheaply (Hobsbawm, 1968; North, 1961; Woodman, 1968; Woodruff, 1973, 1975).

New York was the financial and commercial center. It was heavily tied to both England and the South, much as the Northern German states were tied to England and the Junkers. For New York provided the whole range of financial and marketing arrangements for the Southern cotton crop, and it controlled the import of manufactured goods from England into the United States. New York banks and financial centers were heavily tied to and dependent on British banks, and it was through this link that the United States monetary structure was itself heavily dependent on the British monetary system. The interests of New York, then, rested on the maintenance of its ties to both England and the South, pushing the New York interests in the direction of free trade and political support for the South.

The East and Northeast were the manufacturing and industrial centers. Eastern manufacturing was increasing steadily from

1840 to 1860, just like that in Germany and most of Europe. It included a thriving domestic textile production in New England.

But, like German industrialists, though they were getting stronger, they were in a precarious position within the world-economy. In 1840, finished manufactures made up 45% of U.S. imports and semi-manufactures made up another 11%; thus, 56% of U.S. imports were in manufacturing. In 1850, these numbers rose to 55%, 13%, and 70%. So the U.S. was heavily dependent on foreign manufacturers, most notably from England. The U.S. was the largest single export market for English manufacturers—most important were wool, iron, and steel. And, as in Germany, English money and English products built and stocked the U.S. railroad expansion (Gallman and Hale, 1971; Hobsbawm, 1968; North, 1961; Pierce, 1965; Woodruff, 1975).

Although Britain's major world export was cotton textiles, the United States never took more than a fraction of this product. This was because New England textiles were very early competitive with Britain's in the most important area of the coarser cloths, and Britain could not penetrate the U.S. textile market in this area. Britain exported mainly the finer cloths and fancier prints to the United States. A measure of the success of the New England textile industry was that after 1825, domestic cotton consumption increased at the same rates as Britain's consumption. But U.S. textile producers could not compete with Britain in foreign markets (Potter, 1960).

Through the 1840s and 1850s, then, United States industrial production was increasing, but it was still relatively localized, dependent on British capital, and relatively weak in the world-economy as a whole. The interests of much of this industrial and manufacturing class (with the important exception of textile producers) lay in policies of economic protection and economic nationalism to combat the competitive economic pressures from Britain. Thus, their interests lay in opposite directions from those of the South and New York.

This description of these three regional economic areas is very similar to the previous description of Germany. The major difference in the United States was the existence of a fourth area of small independent farmers in the West. In the West, grain was the major cash crop, and it was highly productive. From 1840 to 1854, there was a 33% growth in agricultural output due to increases in productivity and to the push into new lands. The United States was very early almost self-sufficient in food staples, and the West soon became an area of agricultural export to Europe. By 1840 one-quarter of British imports from the United States were grain and corn. The West's wheat exports to England were surpassed only by the export of Prussian rye until 1846 and the repeal of the Corn Laws. After 1846, the United States became the main supplier of all grains to Britain (Ginzberg, 1936; Hobsbawm, 1968; Schmidt, 1918). United States wheat was becoming more and more central to the world market, and the expansion of new areas for wheat production came to move into rhythm with worldwide demand and price fluctuations (North, 1961). As with any group of agricultural exporters, the interests of the Western grain producers tended toward free trade for the opening of foreign markets and for the ability to buy manu-factures as cheaply as possible. These interests tended to ally the West with the South for much of the 1840s and 1850s. But as Western grain became more important in the world economy and the area for grain cultivation began to increase, Western farmers and Southern planters came into political conflict over the use of Western lands for grain or cotton. Thus, it was the worldwide success of both cotton and grain that tended to move the West and South in somewhat opposite political directions and create enough of a political split to make Western farmers a crucial part of the Republican Party in 1860. Added to this was the fact that from 1840 to 1860, Western trade became more linked to the North than to the South. Western trade with the South did not decrease in the 1850s (this was the golden age of the Mississippi trade), but the growing volume of Western foodstuffs and mining products were going East.

By 1860, the area of the United States exhibited a classic internal division of labor, and economic production in all regions was thriving. But it was also an economy almost totally tied to and dependent on external markets and prices for both grain and cotton, and with an industrial and manufacturing sector that was relatively weak internationally and threatened by Britain.

As in Germany, the landed classes of the South were politically dominant throughout the 1840s and 1850s, through their domination of the Democratic Party and control over the presidency. This political dominance tended to put the interests of free trade and dependence on Britain of the South and New York into a position of political dominance. United States tariffs, which had been relatively protectionist from 1832 to 1847, began a general downward decline until the Civil War reversed this trend. Throughout the 1850s, the agrarian classes were politically dominant, but, just as in Germany, worldwide economic trends tended to increase the economic power of the industrialists relative to the Southern planters within the United States. The Western farmers were also increasing in economic importance, and their political interests were somewhat split: as agricultural exporters they tended to ally with the South over free trade and ties with Britain; but the domestic competition over the expansion of cereal or cotton into new lands tended to put them into opposition with the South and shift their political support to the Eastern manufacturing and industrial classes.

THE UNITED STATES CIVIL WAR

These divergent political and economic interests clashed in the Civil War. The Civil War, like all wars, is not simply a struggle between clearly different interests, for wars tend to expand to involve a whole range of interests. Particularly, it is not correct to characterize the Republican Party from 1856 to 1860 as the party of industrialists or capitalists. As Foner has shown, the party comprised a political coalition of small entrepreneurs in the North, small farmers in the West, and some industrial interests, particularly iron and steel. Since the North (with the exception of New York) and the South had relatively divergent interests, the West came to possess the swing votes in national elections and in Congress. It had been a South-West alliance that had dominated American politics throughout the 1840-1860 period. But in the later part of the 1850s, as we have seen, the coalition between the South and West began to come apart under the combined pressures for control of new Western lands and the increase of Western trade with the north. The Republican Party was the political vehicle for forming the emerging North-West alliance. It was a truly political coalition, and one that required considerable skill to create and mobilize with its patchwork program of "free soil, free labor, and free men" (Foner, 1970; Moore, 1966). By 1860, the pace of Western grain expansion seems to have developed enough that a sufficient number of Western voters entered the Republican Party alliance with the North to enable the party narrowly to capture the presidency from the Democratic Party and the South.

Still, the general forces leading to the Civil War in 1861-1865 were much the same as led to German Unification in 1862-1865. In both cases, a politically dominant agrarian class was faced with a rising industrial class, which was doing well economically but was politically disadvantaged in the state. Though both Junkers and cotton planters prospered in the late 1850s, the worldwide trends favored the producers of the industrial commodities, as the shift in the terms of trade in the 1850s made clear. Hence both agrarian groups needed to maintain political supremacy to maintain their positions. The industrial classes, while becoming stronger relative to their respective agrarian classes, were weak in relation to both the world market and, particularly, Britain. They needed to protect their national markets, especially iron and steel, from British competition, and to become competitive in the world market, not just the local market. For both groups, their interests lay in political control of the state structures.

Moore, then, is basically correct when he argues that the major cause of the Civil War was political and it was fought over control of the state. For the divergent economic interests of the different groups required political solutions, and there is only one state. Hence, the different interests came to conflict over control of the state structure. As in Germany, the United

States political transformation began at the time when the industrial and the politically dominant agrarian class were becoming equalized in power, and at such times political power is crucially important for the future maintenance of economic position.

Why this situation resulted in war in the U.S. but political compromise in Germany is a separate question; but one not hard to answer when one compares the state structures of the two areas. Moore himself found the fact that war had to occur as puzzling. But in Germany, the Junkers could maintain much of their political power and dominance because they were ensconced in the strongly developed and institutionalized civil and military bureaucracy. In the 1850s and 1860s, the U.S. possessed no equivalent developed bureaucracy with institutionalized ties to certain groups (Crenson, 1975; White, 1954). Political supremacy rested largely with the control over the presidency that the South, through the Democratic Party, had maintained for 20 years. Hence, when the South lost the presidency (and much of Congress, if the West was to vote with the North), they lost their major mechanism of political supremacy, and they immediately seceded. Recall that the South did not even wait until Lincoln's program was out, for they no longer had any stable base of political advantage within the state. In Germany, however, the political position of the Junkers was better because of their control over the bureaucracy, and they were able to be dragged unwillingly into a political compromise with the liberals and industrialists. Though they lost some economic and political control, they knew they could not lose all. Hence, the structural situation leading to the conflict was the same in Germany and the United States, but that compromise occurred in Germany and war in the U.S. was a function of the existence of a well-developed bureaucracy in Germany which insured the Junkers some continuing political leverage within the state.

Many analysts of the Civil War also do not understand what the Northern manufacturing and industrial classes had to gain. For they point out that industrialization within the United States was proceeding well throughout the 1850s, in spite of

Southern dominance of the federal government. But as we have argued, the economic competition to Northern industry lay not in Southern agriculture but in British industry. When viewed from the internal perspective, United States industry seems dominant; but when viewed from the world economy, its position was potentially precarious. For it is the nature of economic competition in the world-economy to undercut those economic producers whose area of dominance is restricted locally. To secure their local position, producers also have to expand in the world-economy as a whole. For the Northern industrial and manufacturing interests, Southern control of the federal government was a major obstacle to such economic expansion. A similar situation affected the South and West. For in the 1850s, both cotton and grain production were expanding. But, again, the arena of economic action for these commodities was the world market, and political control of the state apparatus was important for the maintenance of the economic position of these groups too. Thus, it was the role of the areas of the United States in the world-economy which tended to create divergent economic and political interests and create the conditions for conflict over control of the state.

RECONSTRUCTION AND POLITICAL TRANSFORMATION, 1865-1880

In discussing the significance of the Civil War and Reconstruction for political transformation in the United States, we find that this period was characterized by the same three political conditions as in Germany: the economic interests of the industrial class were institutionalized within the state, the United States economy became nationalized and politically protected, and the dominant economic producing groups came to form a political and economic coalition. The two crucial issues to discuss during this period are, first, the institutionalization of industrial and manufacturing interests within the federal government and, second, the maintenance of the North-West alliance.

What the Republican Party and the Civil War accomplished was *politically* to forge a North-West alliance. With the South out of the federal government during the Civil War, many parts of the industrialists' political program were enacted. But the North-West alliance was always considered tenuous by most contemporaries, and a major political program facing Northern groups was how to maintain this alliance after the war. For there was considerable apprehension that with the South back in the Union, the older South-West alliance would be recreated and the North would lose the advantages it had gained during the war (Beale, 1958; Sharkey, 1959; Stampp, 1965; Woodward, 1951).

The coalition between the West and North in 1856-1860 was indeed tenuous. The West was in a somewhat contradictory position. As an area producing a cash crop for export, its interests tended to favor free trade in order to maintain access to foreign markets and to be able to buy cheaper manufactures. Thus, its role in the world-economy in relation to foreign markets made it the natural ally of the South on many issues. But in the 1850s and the 1860s both wheat and cotton production were expanding because of worldwide demand and the desire of both wheat farmers and cotton planters to expand into Western lands brought the two groups into conflict. Thus, from domestic competition for new land, the West and South came to have somewhat opposing interests. It seems that the North-West alliance was created as much from this negative fact that the West-South alliance was breaking down over the issue of the new lands as from any positive pull due to benefits of a North-West alliance. Most observers have argued that the North-West alliance occurred because the North, with its greater population and wealth, was consuming an increasing amount of Western foodstuffs. This was undoubtedly true; but the important question is whether this would have been any different if the West had remained politically allied with the South. The answer is undoubtedly no; for Northern consumers would certainly not have shifted to Prussian or Russian grain, the other alternatives. The point is that the Western grain trade with the North would have continued because of economic necessity, no matter what political alliance was formed. It seems, then, that the North-West alliance was indeed tenuous since it was formed more in opposition to the South over new lands rather than out of mutual benefit between the West and North. The process that served to maintain this North-West alliance during Reconstruction is a major issue to analyze. But first we must discuss the process by which the industrial and manufacturing interests were institutionalized within the federal government.

The claim that the Civil War and Reconstruction created the political dominance of the industrial and manufacturing classes is one of the great controversies in the historical interpretation of this period. This claim is known as the Beard-Beale thesis, after the two major historians who laid the framework for this interpretation.

It is clear, however, that one consequence of the Reconstruction period was the political victory for much of the economic program of the industrial and manufacturing classes. This program included a protective tariff which reversed the downward trend on tariffs imposed by the South in the 1840-1860 period; a new national banking system and a sound paper currency in national bank notes secured by government bonds; federal subsidies for internal improvements, especially railroads; and the sale of mineral and timber resources on government land to private enterprise; and the general expansion of the power and authority of the federal government (Beale, 1958; Moore, 1966; Stampp, 1965; Woodward, 1951). This represented an economic program which was almost identical to that created in Germany at the same time. It was through the enactment of such a program during Reconstruction that the interests of the industrial and manufacturing classes became institutionalized within the state.

Many critics argue, however, that the Reconstruction era should not be interpreted within this framework of the Beard-Beale thesis; and this more recent critique has led to a large amount of confusion. Those Reconstruction historians who question this interpretation make the following argument. They do not argue that Reconstruction did not enact the political program of the industrialists, for we have seen above that it did. Rather, they argue that one cannot describe a unified capitalist class as being the motive force for this program. Such critics as Cobden (1969), Sharkey (1959), and Stampp (1965) have shown that there was no unified capitalist class interest; and on many issues the capitalist groups were opposed. It is criticisms such as this that have been used to deny the economic significance of the Civil War and Reconstruction. Although these specific criticisms are correct, they, in fact, miss the most basic point that the Civil War was not just about the dominance of the capitalist class over the landed class of the South, but a struggle among different *capitalist* interests. As we have seen, the major conflict leading to the war was the conflict between those groups of capitalist producers that were aligned with Britain and whose interests rested with maintaining the United States within its previous position in the world division of labor, and those producing classes whose interests were threatened by British dominance and therefore aimed to break their dependence on Britain and change the position of the United States in the world division of labor. Just as this was the major split leading to the war, it also became the major conflict during Reconstruction.

For example, in studying such issues as the currency contraction, the issue of greenbacks, and the tariff, historians such as Cobden, Sharkey, and Stampp point out that many big capitalist groups opposed the issuance of greenbacks, the creation of a national banking system, and the increase in tariffs. But the groups that opposed these issues, as Sharkey's (1959) own analysis shows, were primarily the financial and commercial interests centered in or tied to New York; and those that favored these issues were primarily the national industrial producers, notably iron and steel, whose interests were threatened by British production. And that split represents exactly the divergent interests that were opposed before the Civil War. For the financial and commercial interests in New York were tied to England, and the national producers were those groups attempting to break such a dependency on England. It is indeed incorrect to interpret this period as one of big capital versus a Southern landed elite and small entrepreneurs; for the basic conflict was between the *national* producers and those producers tied to England. We should, then, expect exactly the split on the issues that has been found by the critics of the Beard-Beale thesis.

Similarly, such historians show that New England textile manufacturers were not protectionist during Reconstruction; and then such critics argue against the economic interpretation of the Civil War. But there is no problem here when we remember that New England textile manufactures had achieved a competitive advantage over England within the United States market by 1840. They were not threatened by British competition at home and so had no need of protection. In fact, these textile producers were preparing to try to compete with Britain in the world market, and for this push they favored free trade in order to secure Indian surat cotton, which had become cheaper than United States cotton (Cobden, 1969).

Many of the seeming paradoxes in the economic interpretation of the Civil War and Reconstruction are straightforwardly explained when one keeps in mind that the issues and the conflicts were not about capitalist producers versus noncapitalist agricultural producers. For the issues and conflicts were essentially between *national* producers threatened by competition with England and those producers whose interests rested in complementary relationships with England.

A major consequence of the Reconstruction period was the political institutionalization of the economic program of the national economic producers. This victory was accomplished through the dominance of the Republican Party in the period 1865-1876. But this victory of the national industrial and manufacturing groups is only part of the significance of this period for the subsequent rise of the United States to core status. As in Germany, we must also realize that what occurred during this period was also a political and economic convergence between these industrial interests and the major agricultural producers. And the crux of this convergence was the maintenance of the alliance between the Northern industrial interests and the Western wheat farmers. For during Reconstruction it was the maintenance of this alliance which allowed for the political victory of the national producers by keeping the South out of the federal government and Congress.

How this alliance was maintained and forged is best illustrated by the conflict over currency contraction and the issuance of greenbacks that provided the first political test of the alliance after the Civil War. The McCulloch policy of currency contraction was initially supported by both manufacturers and the New York financial and commercial interests. But the deflationary consequences of currency contraction quickly proved bad for the national manufacturers, and they shifted to a policy favoring currency expansion and "soft" money. When the manufacturers shifted their position, the policy of currency contraction failed (Sharkey, 1959). The conflict over currency contraction was essentially a conflict between the national producers and the New York financial and commercial interests.

Sharkey notes that the high protectionist Republicans like Henry Carey, Thaddeus Stevens, and William Kellogg were also soft-money supporters; and he sees this as paradoxical because of the support of the big banking and commercial interests for hard money. But there was no contradiction between supporting both protection and soft money, because a rising premium on gold which was fostered by the increase in legal tender notes was the same as increased protection for American manufacturers. A falling premium, as fostered by McCulloch's policy of contraction, represented decreased protection for American manufacturers and an active inducement to the importation of foreign manufactures (Sharkey, 1959). That the New York banking interests should organize to support the policy of contraction was perfectly understandable since their economic position lay with their financial and commercial links to Britain. That they should be opposed by domestic manufacturers who organized for soft money is also understandable, since their interests lay in protection and independence from Britain. An added reason was that soft money, the expansion of the greenbacks, meant greater *national* control of the United States monetary system. For hard money meant greater and more direct dependence of the U.S. monetary system on the British, through their control over gold premiums in the international financial system.

The conflict over currency contraction clearly showed that the divergent forces that had led to the war were still active. As long as the South remained out of the national politics, the national industrial producers were politically stronger than the commercial and financial interests tied to Britain, unless the West allied with this latter group. What was the position of the Western farmers during this debate? As Sharkey shows, they stayed neutral on the currency issue. As we have seen, the position of the Western farmers was contradictory, in that they were pulled in one direction by internal economic reasons and in another by foreign economic reasons. As agricultural exporters they could be expected to align with the New York interests and resist tariff increases. But as small farmers, they could also be expected to favor soft money; since soft money meant (potentially at least) easier credit, lower real interest rates, and the nationalization of the United States monetary system.

What seems to be the crucial reason which kept the West from splitting with the national manufacturers was that grain production and foreign sales were exceptionally high during this crucial period. From 1851 to 1860, wheat exports accounted for 10% of all U.S. exports. But in 1861 to 1870, wheat and wheat products jumped to 21% of all U.S. exports. Prices were also extremely high during this period (Woodruff, 1973, 1975). So with their international economic position being so prosperous, the Western farmers had little to fear from the protectionist and anti-British policies of the industrial and manufacturing classes. Thus they stayed neutral during the currency crisis and continued their political alliance with the North within the Republican Party. This political alliance, then, formed the Reconstruction policy and kept the South out of national politics during the era, and hence allowed the national producers to institutionalize their economic program.

So it was exceedingly prosperous times for Western grain in the world-economy between 1865 and 1873 that cemented the alliance with the national industrial producers. Just as it was changes in the world wheat market that brought Western grain to Europe and forced the Junkers into a policy of

agricultural protection and alliance with the German industrialists, so it was the same conditions that produced the
alliance between the United States grain producers and the
industrialists in the United States. Between 1865 and 1879,
changes in the world wheat market had operated to create a
"marriage of iron and rye" on both sides of the Atlantic. The
political and economic coalition that created modern Germany,
then, was also the political and economic coalition that
created the modern United States.[5]

The final element in the convergence of the major producing
groups in the United States was the South. After the Civil War,
Southern cotton had become less central to the world-economy
as new areas of supply were opened in India and Egypt. But
Southern cotton production and exports were still important
and prosperous. Stampp points out that once the political
position of the Republicans was secured, they rejected Southern
land reform, abolished the Freedman's Bureau, and ended their
political alliance with Southern blacks and small farmers and
tenants. Northern business interests began looking for investment opportunities in the South, and the Republicans began
to appeal to the aristocratic propertied elements in the South.
With the Depression of 1873, northern business wanted
Southern conservatives back into national politics both to
maintain control over labor and to open up business opportunities in the south. The Hays election of 1877 represented
the symbolic culmination of this thrust and the end of Reconstruction. For with the election of Hays and the end of Southern
Reconstruction, all of the dominant economic producers in the
different regions became realigned into what Stampp has
incisively labelled as a truly *national* upper class.

The consequence of Reconstruction was the institutionalization of the economic interests of the national producers, the
breaking of dependence on Britain and the nationalization of
the United States economy, and the convergence of all the
major producing groups into a political and economic coalition
that was to dominate the federal government. The Reconstruction era did not destroy the Southern landed classes; rather it
changed their relative power within the federal government.

Southern political overrepresentation in the state was to continue for another hundred years. The significance of Reconstruction was that it created convergence among previously opposing political and economic interests. With the formation of this national coalition supporting the state, the United States, like Germany, was able to enter a period of aggressive nationalist development which enabled it to outstrip other countries and made it into a core power.

Some analysts argue that since industrialization was proceeding so well before the Civil War, the consequences of the war for the economic development of the United States are questionable. This view has even produced some influential arguments that the Civil War may even have retarded industrialization (Cochran, 1964; Engerman, 1971). But as Barrington Moore has pointed out, such reasoning is blindly narrow minded for it neglects any attention to the political and institutional conditions for development. As we argued before, such a view also neglects the weak position of United States manufactures in the world-economy as a whole. This view also fails to grasp what must be considered one of the most crucial conditions for a country to become a core power, and that is that such development requires a significant political push which is impossible to maintain when significant producing groups within an area are politically and economically opposed.

POLITICAL TRANSFORMATION
IN THE 19TH CENTURY

By 1880 the basic process of political transformation had been accomplished in Germany and the United States. What had been created during the previous 40 years was the forging of the economic coalitions that were to make these two countries into core powers. This process was a function of economic change in the world-economy as a whole and the relationships of the areas of Germany and the United States to that world-economy. From 1640 to 1840, the landed classes had been both economically and politically dominant throughout most of the world-system. But with the start of the 19th century, changes in the world-economy occurred which slowly shifted the locus of economic advantage to the producers of industrial goods. By 1840 the relative economic power of the landed and industrial classes was equalized in many areas, but political power still rested with the former group. The political upheavals in Germany and the United States in mid-century represented the challenge of industrial producers to the political dominance of the agrarian producers. For though industrial production was increasing, the economic position of these industrial producers was still weak and tenuous in relation to the dominance of Britain. The political challenge in these two areas was necessitated by the fact that the landed classes existed in a complementary economic relationship with Britain, and political control of their local states represented the only way for these industrial producers to breka their dependence on Britain and secure their position in the changing world division of labor.

For those areas that were to become core powers, the political transformation rested in the political institutionalization of the economic interests of the industrial producers, the freeing of their economies from the dominance of the British through mechanisms of nationalization and protection, and the forging of a coalition among the major producing groups in the area. The formation of these coalitions was made possible only in those areas where changes in the world-economy as a whole forced those groups with previously diverging interests to come to have convergent economic and political interests. The importance of this convergence was that it created a coalition which supported the state in a program of aggressive nationalist development.

The nature of this political transformation was important in several respects. First, it not only involved a convergence of the interests of dominant agricultural and industrial classes, but focused them on the necessity of a strong state. Second, it institutionalized within the state the interests of the industrialists, who were emerging as the major resource-controlling group in the world-economy. Third, by also institutionalizing the interests of the dominant agricultural producers, it insured that their national economies could rely on domestic rather than imported foodstuffs, a condition which seems necessary for areas attempting nationalist development. And finally, by establishing the political conditions for economically *balanced* nationalist development, these political transformations provided these states with the fiscal infrastructure that underlay their rise to the core of the world-system.

NOTES

1. The figures on changes in landownership are from Hammerow, 1966, and Rosenberg, 1958. For the terms of trade, see Atallah, 1958, and Morgan, 1959.
2. On the relationship between the Prussian bureaucracy and the Junkers, see Gillis, 1968; Hammerow, 1966; Rosenberg, 1958; and Taylor, 1962.
3. On the weak international position of German industrialization, see Borchardt, 1973; Clapham, 1966; Crouzet, 1972; and Woodruff, 1973.
4. For the best description of this whole process, see Gerschenkron, 1943. Also see Moore, 1966.
5. That the Junkers controlled grain production in Germany and free farmers controlled grain production in the United States had the consequence of creating very different political regimes in the future, as Moore's analysis makes clear.

REFERENCES

ATALLAH, M.K. (1958). The long-term movement of the terms of trade between agricultural and industrial products. Rotterdam: Netherlands Economic Institute.
BEALE, H. (1958). The critical year. New York: Frederick Ungar.
BLACK, C. et al. (1975). The modernization of Japan and Russia. New York: Free Press.
BORCHARDT, K. (1973). "Germany 1700-1914." In C.M. Cipolla (ed.), The Fontana economic history of Europe: The emergence of industrial societies-I. London: Collins.
CLAPHAM, J.H. (1966). Economic development of France and Germany 1815-1914. Cambridge: Cambridge University Press.
COBDEN, S. (1969). "Northeastern business and radical reconstruction: A reexamination." In K. Stampp and L. Litwack (eds.) Reconstruction: An anthology of revisionist writings. Baton Rouge: Louisiana State University.
COCHRAN, T. (1964). "Did the Civil War retard industrialization?" In H. Scheiber (ed.), United States economic history. New York: Knopf.
CRENSON, M. (1975). The federal machine. Baltimore: Johns Hopkins University Press.

CROUZET, F. (1972). "Western Europe and Great Britain: 'Catching up' in the first half of the nineteenth century." In A.J. Youngson (ed.), Economic development in the long run. New York: St. Martin's.

ENGERMAN, S. (1971). "The economic impact of the Civil War." In R. Fogel and S. Engerman (eds.), The reinterpretation of American economic history. New York: Harper and Row.

FEILDEN, K. (1969). "The rise and fall of free trade." In C.J. Bartlett (ed.), Britain pre-eminent. New York: St. Martin's.

FISHER, W. (1963). "Government activity and industrialization in Germany." In W.W. Rostow (ed.), The economics of take-off into sustained growth. Cambridge: Cambridge University Press.

FOGEL, R. and ENGERMAN, S. (1974). Time on the cross: The economics of American Negro slavery. Boston: Little, Brown.

FONER, E. (1970). Free soil, free labor, free men. New York: Oxford.

GALLMAN, R. and HALE, E. (1971). "Trends in the structure of the American economy since 1840." In R. Fogel and S. Engerman (eds.), The reinterpretation of American economic history. New York: Harper and Row.

GERSCHENKRON, A. (1943). Bread and democracy in Germany. Berkeley: University of California Press.

GILLIS, J. (1968). "Aristocracy and bureaucracy in nineteenth-century Prussia." Past and Present, 41:105-129.

——— (1970). "Political decay and the European revolutions, 1789-1848. World Politics, 22:344-370.

GINZBERG, E. (1936). "The economics of British neutrality during the American Civil War." Agricultural History, 10:147-156.

HAMMEROW, T. (1966). Restoration, revolution, reaction: Economics and politics in Germany, 1815-1871. Princeton: Princeton University Press.

——— (1969). The social foundations of German unification 1858-1871. Princeton, N.J.: Princeton University Press.

HENDERSON, W.O. (1961). The industrial revolution in Europe. Chicago: Quadrangle.

——— (1965) Britain and industrial Europe 1750-1870. London: Leicester University.

HOBSBAWM, E. (1968). Industry and empire. Middlesex: Penguin.

——— (1975). The age of capital. London: Weidenfeld and Nicolson.

HOFFMANN, W. (1963). "The take-off in Germany." In W.W. Rostow (ed.), The economics of take-off into sustained growth. Cambridge: Cambridge University Press.

MOORE, B. (1966). Social origins of dictatorship and democracy. Boston: Beacon.

MORGAN, T. (1959). "Long-run terms of trade between agriculture and manufacturing." Economic Development and Cultural Change, 8:1-23.

NORTH, D. (1961). The economic growth of the United States 1790 to 1860. Englewood-Cliffs, N.J.: Prentice-Hall.

PIERCE, H. (1965). "Foreign investment in American enterprise." In D. Gilchrist and W.D. Lewis (eds.), Economic change in the Civil War era. Greenville: Eleutherian Mills-Hagley Foundation.

POTTER, J. (1960). "Atlantic economy, 1815-1860: the U.S.A. and the Industrial Revolution in Britain." In L.S. Pressnell (ed.), Studies in the Industrial Revolution. London: Athlone.

ROSENBERG, H. (1958). Bureaucracy, aristocracy and autocracy. Boston: Beacon.

SCHMIDT, L. (1918). "The influence of wheat and cotton on Anglo-American relations during the Civil War." Iowa Journal of History and Politics, 16:400-439.

SHARKEY, R. (1959). Money, class, and party: An economic study of Civil War and Reconstruction. Baltimore: Johns Hopkins University Press.

SKOCPOL, T. (1976). "France, Russia, China: A structural analysis of social revolutions." Comparative Studies in Society and History, 18:175-210.

STAMPP, K. (1965) The era of Reconstruction 1865-1877. New York: Vintage.

TAYLOR, A.J.P. (1962). The course of German history. New York: Capricorn.

TRIMBERGER, E. (1972). "A theory of elite revolutions." Studies in Comparative Economic Development, 7:191-207.

WALLERSTEIN, I. (1974). The modern world-system. New York: Academic.

WHITE, L. (1954). The Jacksonians: A study in administrative history, 1829-1861. New York: Macmillan.

WOODMAN, H. (1968). King cotton and his retainers. Lexington: University of Kentucky Press.

WOODRUFF, W. (1973). "The emergence of an international economy, 1700-1914." In C.M. Cipolla (ed.), The Fontana economic history of Europe: The emergence of industrial societies—II, London: Collins.

——— (1975). America's impact on the world. New York: John Wiley.

WOODWARD, C.V. (1951). Reunion & reaction. Boston: Little, Brown.

Chapter 3

FASCISM AND WORLD ECONOMY

Walter L. Goldfrank

The worldwide transition to socialism continues, with recent victories of socialist movements and parties in Indochina and Southern Africa, and trends toward the left in Southern Europe. Yet a spectre haunts us, in reality as well as in memory: the spectre of facism. If the forces of socialism have made great gains in the last decade, so have they suffered grave setbacks in Southern South America and Southeast Asia. The repressive regimes of Iran and South Korea, of the Central African Republic and Equatorial Guinea, of Guatemala and Nicaragua, all bespeak the ongoing strength of dictatorships with at least some fascist coloration. Note as well the revelations of COINTELPRO activities in the United States—illegal searches, political provocateurs—giving credence to such conceptions as the "dual state." The racist right is growing in England. In the USSR, we see renewed crackdowns on political and ethnoregional dissent. And from the People's Republic of China, an editorial denouncing the so-called Gang of Four accuses them of sabotaging the railways so that the trains

Author's Note: Thanks are due the Research Committee of U.C. Santa Cruz for financial support, the Comparative History Seminar for encouragement and criticism, and Susan Kay Sloan for research assistance.

do not run on time. With street fighting erupting among left- and right-wing Italian students in the original homeland of fascist success, we face more than a spectre.

In what sense are we justified in calling contemporary anti- communist dictatorships "fascist"? Is the word more than a nasty name for the world left to sling at its enemies? As the world economy stagnates and perhaps heads for a serious depression (via, say, unstable currencies and Third World defaults triggering massive bank failures) must we fear the resurgence of fascism in the advanced industrial countries, or its spread throughout more and more of the world? What can we learn from the last long period of economic stagnation and fascist prominence in the world, the period between the wars? Then, too, the cases were different: Germany, Japan, Italy; Spain and Portugal; Chiang's China; Romania, Hungary, Austria, Slovakia, the Ukraine; perhaps Brazil and Argentina, to name the best known. In the last 15 years a great outpouring of research (with gaps to be sure) and interpretations has made it possible to ask these political questions and to attempt a synthetic answer to them.

But the subject of fascism has more than political relevance. At a moment in social science when both conventional liberal and orthodox Marxist paradigms are increasingly called into question, fascism and the fascist era can serve as a strategic site for interpretation and conceptualization. The premise and aim of this essay is that the world-systems perspective, as yet unpolished though it is, can help us at once integrate the best of the older paradigms and overcome their deficiencies. This perspective allows us to proceed in several ways. First, it points to the whole: a contracting world economy causing grave dislocations for many social groups, and a disintegrating international political order with Britain on the decline, a semi-isolationist United States, and a palpable if still long-run threat to capitalism in the existence of the Soviet state.

Second, the world-systems perspective offers the possibility of systematic comparative analysis (Wallerstein, 1974a, and 1974b). Using the concepts of core, semi-periphery, and periphery, we can begin to account for the differences between fascist and nonfascist occurrences. And we can compare the various fascisms among themselves, from the feeble sects of Britain and France and the conservative authoritarianism of Portugal all the way to the Nazi movement and regime. The aim of that regime was no less than the construction of an alternate world-system under German hegemony, stretching from aluminum plants fueled by cheap Norwegian hydro-electric power to a newly enserfed Russian peasantry growing grain under German masters. The very history of that regime recapitulates, in a grotesque and deadly parody, 400 years of capitalism, complete with slavery and plunder, expansion through conquest, forced population movements, recalcitrant labor forces, the destruction of traditional status groups, and the strenthening of a centralized state.

Third, the sources of dynamism in the world-systems perspective seem to me precisely the right ones with which to understand fascism: capital accumulation (class struggle) and interstate competition. With its appeal to the nation as the primary focus of loyalty, fascism commends itself as a phenomenon around which the interaction of class and national forces can be examined. As Perry Anderson (1976) understates it in the postscript to his *Considerations on Western Marxism*, Marx and his followers have seriously misunderstood nationalism, while a world-systems perspective expects it. In this connection it is no accident that World War I should have ushered in the fascist era, for in that war workers of all countries fought, rather than uniting, and found they had more to lose than their chains.

In addition, we can account for concrete international linkages, such as Italian and German sponsorship of fascist movements and regimes in other countries, as well as the way certain regimes, forewarned, were able to forestall the growth of fascism.

The world-system perspective, then, permits a grasp on the whole, suggests intelligible comparisons, understands nationalism as a normal phenomenon. What follows in this essay are two main parts. The first offers two clarifications, outlining in turn the *phases* of fascism as in a "natural history" and the most prominent *theories* of fascism, both liberal and Marxian. The second applies the world-systems perspective in an attempt to reinterpret the various fascist phenomena of the interwar period. At the end, I return to the theme of the overture, commenting on prospects for the short to medium run by comparing the present conjuncture to that earlier time.

CLARIFYING FASCISM: PHASES AND THEORIES

Fascism defies clear definition. Complex in its own right, its exaltation of the national soul means that each particular national version of fascism adpts peculiarities all its own. In contrast to the varieties of communist parties and states, the differences among the fascisms are mandated, as it were, by nationalist principles rather than mere adaptations to local traditions or political exigencies. The recent spate of publications—monographic, comparative, interpretive—brings us closer to the possibility of consensual clarification, including the difficult question of the degree to which fascism is a unitary phenomenon. The two clarifications proposed in this first part should move us in that direction, saving the cross-national comparisons for later. Logically they go together, for often the various theoretical interpretations speak past one another precisely because theorists are attempting to explain different phases of fascism in the same social formation, or even different social formations themselves.

PHASES

Let me first outline the phases of fascism, phases realized in different degrees in different countries. First was a peculiar European intellectual climate—itself not a national phenomenon—that originated in France but found echoes across the continent. Second came the formation of political sects. Third came movements in the form of political parties, where permitted. Fourth came the stage of regime. At the end, as defeat in war spelled at least a temporary demise of fascism, one could adduce a desperate fifth phase, a regression to sect movement, the Republic of Salo in Italy, the super-barbarous last year of the thousand-year Reich.

Now these are not true stages, in the sense that one cannot exist without the prior one already having existed. So long as one operates on the level of nation-states, they can be skipped. In Norway, for example, Quisling's Nasjonal Samling was a sect installed as regime, and the same was true for several of the Eastern European collaborationist governments. Or, in Japan, it seems plausible to call the regime of the late 1930s "fascist," while admitting that the closest thing to a fascist sect was much more traditionalist than any in Europe, and that the Imperial Rule Assistance Association was more a government creation than a mass movement. Or, to take one more set of examples often present in considerations of fascism, in Brazil and Argentina fascist sects, perhaps on the verge of becoming serious movements, were restrained and even destroyed by populist-authoritarian regimes that borrowed something from fascism but were quite distinctive. However, if one thinks in world-system terms, the requiredness of "stage" conceptions is obviated at the nation-state level: we should rather begin to *expect* uneven and combined development, politically as well as economically.

Let me rehearse the phases again, in a little more detail. First was the intellectual climate in the decades around the turn of the century, a climate from which would emerge an ideology at once anti-liberal and anti-Marxist, corporatist yet anti-traditionalist, revolutionizing yet counterrevolutionary, above all nationalist. With its aspiration for discipline, order, and natinal vindication, Boulangism in France was the first important precursor. Some of the strands that went into fascism can be found in Sorel's syndicalist vision, with its emphases on action as opposed to talk, agonistic struggle as opposed to elections and parliaments, brotherhood and comradeship as opposed to association around interests, virile producers as opposed to effete bourgeois, the psychological power of myth as opposed to rational argument. It was an era of irrationalism, of LeBon's psychology of the crowd, of Gobineau's racialism reinforced by Social Darwinism, of Bergson's vitalist philosophy. Freud's discovery of the unconscious, even Durkheim's corporatism and "collective conscience" were at once symptomatic of the breakdown of faith in reason and liberal constitutionalism. (How these intellectual developments connect to the structural changes of those times—the rise of anarchism and of organized socialism, the recurrent crises of capitalism, the interimperialist struggle for colonies, the waning of British hegemony—is another story.) Nationalist doctrines were elaborated as never before, in Germany of course as well as France and Italy, and with repercussions throughout southern and eastern Europe.

This complex of ideas further included anti-Semitism and anti-cosmopolitanism, opposition to international finance as well as to international socialism. For Corradini, Mussolini's most important source, Italy was a "proletarian nation" which had to struggle unremittingly in international politics as well as internally. The state must transcend the vulgar compromising of interests. A new elite—here Pareto and Mosca play their part—must organize the regeneration; and elites, after all, were now proved to be part of the natural order of things. The attacks on parliamentarism and evolutionary socialism were joined by many on the left, not just Sorel. One thinks of Michels' denunciations of the SPD, Lenin's attacks on the spontaneous economism of the masses, Labriola's rage at class-collaborationist socialism. Or, consider the 9th and 10th points of the 1909 Futurist Manifesto: "We want to glorify war—the only cure for the world—and militarism, patriotism, the destructive gesture of the anarchists, the beautiful ideas which kill, and contempt for women. We want to demolish museums and libraries, fight morality, feminism, and all opportunist and utilitarian cowardice" (Sternhill, 1976:344).

Pulling together this nascent ideology in the pre-World War I decade were a number of fascist sects. More sprung up after the war, and in the ensuing years derivative sects emerged in more and more countries. These sects conceived of themselves as both nationalist and socialist; in 1898 during the Dreyfus Affair Maurice Barrès first spoke of "Socialist Nationalism." In 1903 national socialist parties were founded in France and Austria, and in 1904 the Federation Nationale des Jaunes de France. Yellow socialism, at once anti-Semitic and anti-Marxist, had branches in Germany and Switzerland. But in the prewar prosperity nothing much came of these sects. Again after the war fascist sects were formed, particularly in northern Italy, becoming a mass movement under Mussolini's leadership in 1921. Germany was the only other case of sects coalescing into a mass movement, at least until after 1930, when Austria, Hungary (the Arrow Cross), Romania (the Iron Guard), and Spain during the Civil War witnessed such growth. The sect stage of fascism allowed for the purest expression of the ideological elements outlined above: nationalism, anti-conservatism, hostility to "divisive" class struggle and to the bearers of that doctrine, anti-conservatism, anti-parliamentary direct action, and a call for the total undoing of decadent bourgeois society and the remaking of a spiritual, idealistic people's community. The leadership tended to be composed of disillusioned socialist urban intellectuals, the membership of disgruntled veterans, students, and assorted middle-class elements and young workers, often from border areas where nationalist sentiment ran particularly deep.

To draw a precise line between sect and movement presents a measurement problem beyond the scope of this essay. Size, relative to the politically active population, is the most important criterion; political conditions, meaning the degree to which mass participation existed or was tolerated is another. Using electoral statistics (with a 10% cutting point) and impressionistic evidence, my tentative judgment is that only Belgium, the Netherlands, and Slovakia should be added to the brief list above. The Mexican *sinarquistas* claimed half a million supporters at their height in the early forties, and might perhaps deserve inclusion; but most of their impact was restricted to one region. And if most of the sects were relatively harmless and kept in check (for example, the Açao Integralista Brasileira, the Afirmación de una Neuva Argentina, the British Union of Fascists), some decidedly were not (for example, the Croatian Ustacha).

But if precision is at this point difficult, the sense of the classification is not. Compared to sects, movements were more heterogeneous in their social composition, blurred in their ideology, opportunist in their tactics. Combined development was the key, as in the Nazi melange of electoral activity—their organizing work in rural districts was particularly effective—and extralegal violence. In both the Italian and German situations, serious tensions existed within the movements between left and right wings, rural and urban branches. The Italian movement was rather domesticated by coming to power so swiftly, while the Nazis fared very poorly in the fat years from 1925 to 1929. But when the depression hit, their rise was rapid, with an electoral peak of 43% in 1933, one month after Hitler had been installed as chancellor.

It is very important in both the sect and movement phases to see the rationality of fascism, the plausibility of its critiques of the existing order, the appeal of its slogans, if not the possibility of realizing its ultimate visions. Probably because of its barbarous excesses, fascism as a whole has been "labelled," to use that word in its technical sociological sense, as an example of madness or collective psychosis. But intelligent and well-meaning people believed it, supported it, fought for it. On the other hand, with all the compromises and hypocrisies of a prolonged movement phase, the Nazis could not hold together. Success in gaining control of the state was achieved only at the price of purging the left wing, first the Strasser brothers who persisted in aiming at a working-class constituency in 1932, then Rohm and the SA in 1934. For in spite of the repeated attempts to woo the working class away from the socialists and communists, it was the middle strata,

upper as well as lower, rural as well as urban, who provided
the movement's social base, squeezed as they were between
big capital and big labor. And to appease the conservative
right—that other essential ingredient in the fascist success—
it proved useful to jettison parts of the movement and thus
become the regime.

The phase of regime is easier to delimit, entailing the control
of a state and the implementation of specific sorts of policies.
However, even in this formal classification, two important
subtypes must be distinguished. On the one hand are those
fascist regimes which were either the direct creation of successful
fascist movements, like Germany and Italy, or ones in which
fascist movements played an important role, like Spain and
Hungary. On the other hand are those regimes which borrowed
elements of fascist ideology, policy, and practice but which
might also be characterized as authoritarian, whether conservative like Portugal, populist like Argentina, or expansionist
and militarist like Japan. It is with this latter set of regimes
that one runs into arguments with those who prefer a more
restrictive definition of fascism (for one example, see de Felice,
1977). I would argue, however, that the character of international alliances, the strength of anti-communism, the
curtailing of the independent organization of labor, and/or
the attacks on liberalism add up to fascism, if the term is to
have generic meaning.

In the first set of regimes, the movement survived and even
grew, but with compromises and accommodations, disillusion
grew as well. The Italian fascist younger generation of 1935,
for example, was disgusted with what they saw as Mussolini's
abandonment of the glorious ideals, just as others would be
with his acceptance of anti-Semitism and alliance with Hitler.
Yet despite accommodations, in varying degrees there was
also a systematic effort to remake the society, to crush existing
worker organizations and replace them with others, to repress
political opponents by any means necessary, and to use anti-
communism as an attraction for the capitalist democracies.
In the second set of regimes, the movements and sects that

existed were kept on a short leash, if they were permitted to exist at all. But the social and foreign policies of these regimes were roughly comparable to those of the first subtype.

The fifth phase of fascism alluded to earlier needs little further comment. Where movements had come to power, their ultimate downfall required more than the crushing of the armies they came to command. A brief reign of desperate sectarianism ensued, with horrifying consequences. As for echoes of fascism, there were scattered attempts at revival, especially in West Germany in the 1950s, but with little resonance; and neo-fascism has been little more than a minor irritant in Italy, at least until the present. But the Frente Nacionalista Patria y Libertad—the paramilitary right-wing organization that played an important role in the overthrow of the Popular Unity government in Chile—is traceable directly to the Movimiento Nacionalista de Chile, which a group of Nazis and other rightists founded in 1940. Ironic as may be that link across the great postwar boom, it need not detain us; for the purposes of the subsequent analyses, the most important phases are those of sect, movement, and regime.

THEORIES

As suggested earlier, different theories of fascism often talk past one another because they focus on different phases or different countries—typically Italy versus Germany. Although they differ, often sharply, these theories are often complementary rather than contradictory; none may be dismissed out of hand, although all have more limited applicability than is claimed for them. Theories of fascism may be broadly divided into two kinds, liberal and Marxist. Not surprisingly, the liberal theories tend to focus on fascism as ideology, sect, and movement, while the Marxist theories tend to focus on regimes and their effects. Not surprisingly, because liberals worry about their favored political forms: as Lipset puts it, "If we want to preserve and extend parliamentary democracy, we must understand the source of threats to it" (Lipset, 1963:178). Again not surprisingly, because Marxists worry about the proletariat, the communist movement, and the socialist countries. Everywhere the working class, Marxist parties, and the Soviet Union were the chief political enemies of fascist regimes. So liberals focus on threats to parliamentary regimes in the movement phase and the authoritarian or totalitarian curtailment of parliaments and civil liberties insofar as they discuss fascist regimes, thus tarring fascism and communism with the same extremist and dictatorial brushes. Marxists, meanwhile, tend to read intentions and strategies back from the anti-communist, anti-working-class monopoly capitalist regimes, thus tarring liberalism and fascism with the same bourgeois and capitalist brushes. Furthermore, at least until very recently, both liberals and Marxists have tended to deny the originality of fascism, the former seeing it as an aberrant form of mass politics, the latter as the most vicious variant of the capitalist state.

Both liberals and Marxists have contributed to versions of a culture-personality theory which can be passed over rapidly. Perhaps helpful for explaining individual differences in support for or participation in fascist movements, or obedience to fascist regimes, or perhaps even the varying modes of brutality, the culture-personality hypothesis offers little for comparative macro-analytic study, of either the causes or the timing of fascism. One thinks here of Erikson or Benedict among the liberals, painting portraits of authoritarian cultures with which the U.S. happened to be at war. Among the Marxists are Reich and Adorno, with their portrayals of authoritarian families, repressed sexuality, and sadomasochistic personalities. Although the F-scale received its name from fascism, its analytic utility is doubtful.

Let me move quickly through what appear to be the six major structural theories, three liberal, three Marxist. Rarely are they found in pristine form, as they overlap and intersect, often quite explicitly treating different aspects of the fascist era. Note that the three on each side rather mirror one another. They are, on the liberal side, (1) strains in modernization; (2) developmental dictatorship; (3) democratic breakdown;

and, on the Marxist side, (4) culmination of revolution from above; (5) interimperialist rivalry; and (6) reactive class struggle from above.

Several variants exist of the "strains in modernization" interpretation, and they often go together. One, originated by Arendt (1961) and formalized by Kornhauser (1959), stresses the anomie of rapid industrialization and urbanization, the concomitant destruction of traditional ties, and the availability of "the masses" as isolated and defenseless individuals for mobilization by movements and manipulation by regimes. "Déclassés of all classes, unite," might be the slogan. This view works best for interpreting the attraction of fascist sects for the uprooted veterans of World War I, and perhaps for some of the displaced Germans from the Eastern territories given to Poland. It may help explain the rush of first-time voters to the Nazis in the 1932 and 1933 elections. But the Nazis seem rather to have infiltrated and influenced *organizations* in their rise to power, and not been supported by atomized individuals (Linz, 1976:93).

A second variant of the "strains in modernization" theory originated with Parsons (1954) and is echoed by Dahrendorf (1969), who, to be sure, touches most of these theoretical bases in his explanation of Nazism. Here the theme is not so much anomie as cultural lag at the political and ideological levels. The failure of liberalism to take hold, in theory as well as practice, is the key. The persistence of traditional status groups, side by side with advanced capitalist industry, both weakened the middle class and made plausible the Nazi appeal to "reestablish" a people's community of farmers and workers freed from the vulgarity and uncertainty of the market.

Mention of the middle class leads to a third variant of the "strains in modernization" approach, what Lipset (1963, Ch. 5) puts together when he draws on the "status politics" tradition to call fascism the extremism of the center. Here attention centers on the social base: the squeezed "old" middle class (both urban and rural) threatened by the growing power of big capital and big labor, hurt (in Germany) by the inflation of 1923-1924 and panicked by the inability of successive Weimar governments to restore prosperity or order after the depression hit. This variant works best in explaining the electoral base, but even there misses the significant contributions of the "new" middle class and the upper middle class (Hamilton, cited in Linz, 1976:119), contributions which were even more important in analyzing those elements in the leadership who were enamored of the most modern technology.

The second major theoretical approach is to see nationalism as the key explanatory element, and to conceive of fascism as a "developmental dictatorship," the phrase is Gregor's (1974). Here the focus is on the first fascism, Italy, and the analysis based largely on the writings of Corradini and Mussolini. Corporatism becomes the political form, national economic development the principal policy. Class struggle is divisive, internationalism treacherous, parliamentary organization feeble. The maddeningly tendentious Gregor has trouble with Germany—already industrialized—and relishes comparing Stalin, Mao, Castro, and Abbie Hoffman with Mussolini, but no matter. The view is in large measure cogent, seeing fascism as the response of the defeated or disappointed latecomers to industrialization and world power status, or at least as a concerted push for modernization organized by a single party and directed against the interests of the leading world powers. That this view was already stated in all essentials in 1938 by the Romanian engineer and economist, Mihail Manoilescu, may be of interest.

A third major perspective on fascism is more political in focus, the analysis of democratic breakdown. Proposed by the historian Karl Dietrich Bracher (1970), this model centers on the failure of parliamentary regimes in crisis. Legitimacy is weak for various reasons, both left and right extremes attack both the government and the system itself, paramilitary violence is uncontrolled. At the same time the existence of open political competition allows the fascists to organize and electioneer, to make and break alliances, to seek financial support and votes wherever they might find them. Bracher stresses the active deceptions brought off by Hitler, and the many points at which elements of the traditional right unwittingly or knowingly collaborated with him. This model, obviously inapplicable to authoritarian regimes, has clear utility in discussing Italy, Spain, perhaps Japan, and in our own time, Chile. It is a part of the welcome tendency in social science to restore the (relative?) autonomy of the political, so long restricted in both liberal and Marxian frameworks.

The fourth theory is Barrington Moore's (1966) conception of fascism as the "culmination" of revolution from above. In his argument, if in the course of development neither a bourgeois nor a communist revolution destroys the landed aristocracy, what commercial and industrial bourgeoisie there is will make alliances with that "feudal" class; this class will in turn favor both "Catonist" solutions to the social question and expansionist militarism. Weak on the role of the state, this approach mirrors the cultural lag variant of the "strains in modernization" theory. It does not work for the periphery, but then in Moore's terms those countries had not yet taken *any* route to modern society. Nor does it work for Italy, where premodern elements had little to do with the rise or course of fascism.

Fifth comes the Leninist conception of interimperialist rivalry, which mirrors in some ways the idea of developmentalist dictatorship but at a higher stage of development. As Dobb (1963:371-383) states it, the Germans and, by implication, the Japanese (and Italians?) turn to war and fascism to secure materials, markets, and loci for capital exports. Competing with the other capitalist powers yet facing an organized socialist movement at home, war and war psychology to control the workers become the only way out. Hence fascism appears as the highest or last stage of imperialism, itself the highest stage of capitalism. Until the next one.

Such a stage theory reappears in the sixth major explanation of fascism, that of reactive class struggle from above. Again fascism is presented as belonging to imperialism (or "monopoly capitalism"), the "highest" stage of capitalism. "After them, us," said the KPD in one of the more pathetic Marxist attempts at prediction. Two variants of this position exist, the "instrumentalist" scheme of Dimitrov and the Third International, and the "structuralist" interpretation of Poulantzas (1974). Expressed with some subtlety in Franz Neumann's *Behemoth*, the older version posits fascism as the instrument of a desperate monopoly capitalist class. From understating the tensions between state and class even at the height of the regime, this variant reads backwards in time to the intentions and strategies of the monopoly fraction, pointing to evidence like a few industrialists' early financial support for the Nazis, and the somewhat greater support they gave in the depression years. Overlooked is the evidence of greater support for other parties, including the Social Democrats. And was it petite bourgeois self-hatred that led Marxists of said social origin so to deprecate that stratum as to consign its members prematurely to the famous dustbin of history? Nazi electoral gains might well have been preempted by serious left organizing in the countryside.

Conceived as a critique of the Third International's instrumentalist theories and economistic practice, Poulantzas's *Fascism and Dictatorship* is a structuralist fiasco, seriously flawed in theory and method. Claiming to distinguish "real causes" from "secondary features," it rather assumes that class struggle is the real cause of everything. Pretending to analyze fascism as one form of the "exceptional capitalist state" (the others being Bonapartism and military dictatorship), it starts with a theory of the normal capitalist state—if there is such a thing—derived from another exceptional form. If the theory is lame, so is the method. Not only is the vast literature ignored, Germany and Italy—especially Germany—are chosen as cases to illustrate the theoretical theses, since "the characteristics of fascism are clearer and more complete in Nazism than in Italian fascism" (Poulantzas, 1974:14). But this is only the case if one accepts that fascism is what Poulantzas says it is, namely the political mechanism through which the transition from competitive to monopoly capitalism is effected.

Not for nothing do the structuralists claim Freud as a precursor: the state in Poulantzas' theory is not the instrument of a class but rather, like a dream in psychoanalysis, the sublimated expression of the system as a whole. The petite bourgeoisie plays its role as the unwitting instrument of this transition, even becoming the ruling class for a brief moment. Given the Maoist hindsight which Poulantzas applies to the botched politics of the Third International, it is perhaps not surprising that the Germany of his descriptions keeps sounding like the USSR. With the Third International for a foil, it is easy to write a bad book and still come out ahead. (See de Felice, 1977:39-48, for an account of the increasingly unreal Comintern analyses; for an extended critique of Poulantzas, see Rabinbach, 1976a.)

Let me summarize briefly. The liberal theories in one way or another involve strain or the response to strain, some notion of failed or delayed transition, of which fascism, like communism, is a disease. The Marxist theories focus on the working class, the state, above all on the bourgeoisie. In the first instance the bourgeoisie is seen as weak vis-à-vis a state that features significant "pre-bourgeois" elements, and is hence in need of more than parliamentary mediation. In the second the bourgeoisie uses the state to further its class interests in the world. In the third it either uses or is alchemically the beneficiary of a state that represses the working class and organizes the dominance of the monopoly faction. Here the failed transitions of the liberals are concretized into failures of particular national bourgeoisies (and/or particular proletariats) to play their "normal" developmental role—a note struck by Marx for Germany in analyzing 1848—or, in the Leninist variant, into the desperate attempt of those bourgeoisies to do so. All of these approaches have something to offer; as I try out a world-systems perspective on the same data, they and the analyses that embody them will necessarily be echoed. But perhaps the notion of failed *national* transitions between clearly delimited and historically successive stages must be jettisoned.

FASCISM AND THE WORLD-SYSTEM

Let me begin with a few stark propositions. First, fascism was a phenomenon of a stagnating, even contracting, world economy, with excess capacity, serious inflation, high unemployment in the core, and slack demand for the products of the periphery. Second, fascism was engendered by not just *any* contraction but by one that was itself aggravated by the uncertainties and confusions of a hegemonic shift in world politics, from English to United States dominance. As such the period of fascism is a period of war and revolution, like the middle of the 17th century and the decades around 1800. Third, the position and opportunities of different groups in the world-system can account for much of the variation in the differential appeal, success, and consequences of fascism as one of the worldwide currents of that time. Two sets of comparisons are relevant here: comparisons *among* the various fascisms of the core, semi-periphery, and periphery; and comparisons within each analytic zone of the world-system to highlight the similarities and differences of fascist and nonfascist responses to the changing world economy.

However, before attempting to sketch out the plausibility of these propositions, let us briefly recall a contribution to the study of fascism largely ignored by the literature reviewed above—the contribution of Karl Polanyi. Perhaps the most important immediate precursor of the world-systems perspective, Polanyi published *The Great Transformation* (1957) in 1944, at the height of the horror. A justly famous book, it is in one respect consistently misunderstood. Almost every social scientists one asks will say that the transformation referred to in the book's title is the rise and consequences of the market system, the subject of Part II which occupies about three-fourths of the volume. It is an honest mistake; even MacIver makes it in his preface. But no, the "great transformation" refers to the *demise* of the market system, "the transformation of a whole civilization in the thirties" (p. 20), with an utter breakdown of the international economy and a drastic increase in state intervention in most national economies. Polanyi conceived his analysis as the rise and demise of what he called the market system, from 1790 to 1940. What in fact he analyzed was one-plus long cycle, the rise and demise of English hegemony. Suffering from a common Anglo-centric and time bound view of industrialization, he saw neither back past mercantilism nor forward to the time of renewed technical change and of U.S. hegemony. Just the same, his account of fascism in Parts I ("The International System") and III ("Transformation in Progress") is well worth restating.

Polanyi starts out by positing four institutions as responsible for the Hundred Years' Peace of the 19th century: the balance of power, the international gold standard under the aegis of *haute finance*, the self-regulating market with unheard of material welfare, and the liberal state. The bulk of chapter one is devoted to the not-quite-hidden hand of haute finance, the least known of the four institutions, "amphibious" in its bridging of the economic and the political. In Chapter Two, "Conservative Twenties, Revolutionary Thirties," he argues that haute finance was unable to prevent or control the Great Depression, which was above all caused and prolonged by liberal faith in the self-regulating capacities of the market. The description is marvelous, the ultimate explanation rather too idealistic.

Polanyi returns to the theme of breakdown after the memorable excursus on the rise of the market system and the efforts of "society" to protect itself from that system. In the two chapters of Part II, "Self-regulation Impaired" and "Disruptive Strains," he argues for "the constitutive importance of the currency in establishing the nation as the decisive economic and political unit of time" (p. 203). He asserts that "for international purposes the currency was the nation; and no nation could for any length of time exist outside the international scheme" (pp. 205-206). He locates the beginning of the end in the depression of 1873-1896 and the rise of protectionism, which he explains as a response by the Western countries to "the fear of consequences similar to those which the powerless peoples were unable to avert" (p. 214), like agrarian distress among grain growers, or gunboat diplomacy. From competing protectionisms came imperialist rivalry and the subsidization in Germany and the United States of the formation of monopolies.

Then we come to Part III, in which Polanyi analyzes the twenties and thirties again. With contraction the overriding feature,

> Social protection and interference with the currency were not merely analogous but often identical issues. Since the estab-lishment of the gold standard, the currency was just as much endangered by a rising wage level as by direct inflation—both might diminish exports and eventually depress exchanges. [p. 227]

He shows the socially conservative and fiscally "responsible" policies of country after country, and the shifting westward of the burden of currency failures until the great crash in the United States brought the world economy to its knees. The existence of the USSR made workers' parties and movements more "ominous" to capital. Above all,

> The stubbornness with which economic liberals, for a critical decade had, in the service of deflationary policies, supported authoritarian interventionism, merely resulted in a decisive weakening of the democratic forces which might otherwise have averted the fascist catastrophe. Great Britain and the United States—masters not servants of the currency—went off gold in time to escape this peril. [pp. 233-234]

In his penultimate chapter, Polanyi analyzes fascism, which he characterizes as an "escape from an institutional deadlock (between labor and capital) which was essentially alike in a large number of countries," "a reform of the market economy achieved at the price of the extirpation of all democratic institutions, both in the industrial and in the political realm" (p. 237). Fascism had little to do with national causes or national mentalities, and succeeded where it did *not* because

---

of the size of its mass following but because of the "influence of the persons in high position whose good will the fascist leaders possessed, and whose influence in the community could be counted upon to shelter them from the consequences of an abortive revolt, thus taking the risks out of revolution" (p. 238). He calls it a "move" rather than a "movement," because of the abruptness of its appearance and decline in the early twenties, and its sudden reemergence with the depression. It was a "move" that fused with either or both of the main political tendencies of the time, counterrevolution and national revisionism. In the first phase, only Italy's conservatives needed to put fascists in power to secure the counterrevolution. But with the calamity of the depression, and the fact that "Germany's equality of status could not have been attained without a revolutionary departure," fascism soon became "a world power." And in the mid-thirties, while the British were cutting their defense spending to balance the budget and attempting to restore the gold standard, Germany "deliberately cut loose" from the international economy and embarked on the road to autarchy through militarist expansion (pp. 242, 245-246).

In his own way, then, Polanyi also underestimated fascism, refusing even to dignify it as a movement with a coherent ideology. And his causal statements have a monism about them which only detracts from the great value of his approach. Overstatements like the following do not help: "In reality the part played by fascism was determined by one factor: the condition of the market system" (p. 242). There is too little attention to different structures of production in different countries, with the concomitant variation in the effects of the depression. Perhaps, too, the balance of power and the liberal state should not be conceived as "superstructure," with rather more weight going to the active pursuit of interests by states and classes. Yet despite the criticism, *The Great Transformation* remains the fundamental starting point for a world-systems analysis of fascism, as remarkable for its insights as it is for the neglect which others have shown it.

A few more general considerations on stagnation and power shifts can introduce the comparative analysis. For the leading countries of Western Europe in the period 1880-1913, manufactures had increased at an average annual rate of 2% per capita; in the 1913-1938 period, the comparable rate of increase was only .8%. "Europe was suffering from the arteriosclerosis of an old-established, heavily capitalized economic system, inflexible in relation to violent economic change" (Quoted in Dowd, 1955:277). Meanwhile the U.S. GNP, despite the depression, sustained an average annual growth rate of 3.5% for 1879-1938. And Japan made significant gains, with a per capita GNP advance of 32.8% from 1900 to 1929, a growth in percentage of total world manufactures from .6% in 1900 to 3.8% in 1939, and a rise in the share of total manufactured exports from 1.6% in 1899 to 7.5% in 1937. In that last time span the United Kingdom's share fell from 33.8% to 22.4%, France's from 15.1% to 6.1%, while Germany's started at 23.2%, rose to 27.5% on the eve of World War I, fell to 21.9% in 1929, and returned to 23.4% by 1937. The U.S. with its larger territory and population and new plants in the newer industries, experienced a rise from 11.5% in 1899 to 13.0% in 1913, then to 21.4% in 1929, inching off to 20.3% in 1937 (see the tables in Chirot, 1977:97, 104).

In terms of world political economy, Germany's attempt in World War I to attain a hegemonic position within the core at the expense of declining Britain (and France) was thwarted by the United States, which was rising even faster. Fascist Germany would try again. In Asia, Japan was moving from semi-peripheral toward core status; its eventual attempt to displace British, French, and Dutch imperialism in Southeast Asia led to a collision there, again with the United States, which had its own fish to fry. Meanwhile semi-peripheral Russia was becoming the USSR, the first self-proclaimed homeland of socialism in a capitalist world. The struggle for hegemony within the core was by no means settled: with fascism in power in Germany, Japan and semi-peripheral Italy, and socialism in the semi-peripheral USSR, the alliance possibilities were several, as the ideologically confusing shifts before World War II were to prove—Germany against the USSR in Spain, the Nazi-Soviet pact, the Allies-Axis alignment of World War II. (*Then* the Cold War!) Throughout the core and in the rising semi-periphery, state intervention in the economy was the response to world depression, with armament industries leading the way in Germany, Japan, the USSR, and eventually the United Kingdom and the United States. This change in the relationship of state and society was first noted for the capitalist countries in 1935 by the heterodox Marxist Fritz Sternberg, and is crucial for Polanyi, who notes its applicability to the USSR as well.

For the weaker semi-periphery (Spain, Austria, Czechoslovakia, Canada, South Africa, Australia, and perhaps Argentina) and the vast periphery (including Mexico and Brazil which were becoming semi-peripheral by the end of the period), there were disasters and opportunities. Eastern Europe, Spain, Ethiopia, China, and Southeast Asia suffered most. For the rest, with variations to be sure, depressed demand caused dislocations and hardships, with commodity prices falling faster than industrial prices. Chile, for example, lost 80% of its exports between 1928 and 1933! (Kindleberger, 1973:191). Import-substituting industrialization made important gains, and the allied war effort brought renewed demand and rising prices for materials exports (and a call for support against the Axis, including troops). Nationalist movements made great strides, with and without the help and inspiration of the USSR, the Comintern, the European left, and different combatants during the war. Thus the Axis surrender ushered in a wave of decolonization in Asia and the Middle East, and the triumph of the Chinese revolution.

Let me turn now to some brief comparisons of the various fascist phenomena—sects, movements, regimes—in the core, semi-periphery, and periphery. In the core, how do we account for the German trajectory, compared on the one hand to the sects (perhaps movements) in France, the Netherlands, Belgium, the United Kingdom, and the United States, and

on the other hand to the varieties of "New Deal" state intervention and social programs? How do semi-peripheral Japan
(on the way up) and Italy compare with "socialism in one
country" in the USSR? What of the rest of the semi-periphery?
In the periphery, finally, what do we make of the Eastern
European fascism, of Latin America, of the KMT?

CORE

To begin with the core is to begin with Germany. If in his
account of the origins of World War II, A.J.P. Taylor errs
in making Nazi Germany out to be just another great power
seeking its interests in world politics (Mason, 1964), so have
a whole host of analysts gone to the opposite extreme in
portraying Germany between the wars as demonically insane.
The trick in describing and accounting for the rise of the Nazi
movement and also the character of the regime is to see the
changing patterns of convergence of Nazi aims and promises
with the interests of particular groups as the world political
economy contracted. Thus the early Nazi formation among
the uprooted of World War I made great sense to that assort-
ment of displaced easterners, restless and vindictive veterans
first brought together in 1920 in the context of ongoing left-
wing revolutionary attempts and the disastrous settlement
at Versailles. In spite of proscription and later harassment,
the Nazis gained members (if not yet large numbers of voters)
during the fat years of Weimar, 1925 to 1928. From that
point, with propaganda intensified in medium-sized towns
and in the countryside, the Nazis made stunning electoral
advances among the Protestant middle and upper middle
class who doubted the protection of their interests by existing
center and right parties. Simultaneously, the highly capitalized,
"disaccumulative" structure of rationalized German industry
began to suffer in the crisis. Two groups emerged, interna-
tionalists like Siemens who wanted to follow deflationary
policies, have reparations cancelled and remain connected
with the world market, and nationalists like the weaker iron
and steel industry which sought to bail itself out by a revival

of the war economy and hence heavy government spending. The former supported Bruning, the latter turned toward Hitler. But both feared the possible socialization of heavy industry, and at the end of 1932 a regrouping of industrial giants, large landowners, and the military was effected, and the Hitler-Papen cabinet welcomed (Rabinbach, 1974).

Hitler then was able to deceive the conservative right (here are the "feudal remnants" of East German capitalist agriculture) and perhaps many industrialists that his aims dovetailed with their political and economic interests—crushing the independent power of labor at both the shop and party levels, protecting agriculture, reviving the economy through rearmament and expansion (Bracher, 1970). But as Mason (1964) argues, that consensus broke down in 1936: within industry the electrochemical sector led by I.G. Farben gained dominance over iron and steel, industrial interests as a whole fell into disarray, and the primacy of state policy over industry was secured, although short-run profits were never threatened.

Hitler was also able to deceive the British. At the important junctures, his government was treated as merely seeking revisions of Versailles; important elements in England believed that fascism would do what liberal democracy was too decadent to do, contain and beat back Bolshevism, as Barraclough (1967:218-221) puts it. The Anglo-German naval agreement of 1935 was a perfect instrument, as it made Hitler out to be pacific while leaving him room to pursue expansionism on land in Central and Eastern Europe (Watt, 1956).

World War II reveals in acute form the contradictions of the primacy of National Socialist politics, fueled by a vision of a Europe dominated by a racially pure German elite. The economy was not ready for a large and long war, the war aims themselves were ill-conceived, defeat was total; and rather than determining foreign policy, the capitalists followed after Hitler's advances, seizing opportunities to secure new situations in which to profit. At the same time, a German economic empire was created in Europe, in a series of ad hoc measures, perhaps justified by the plausible theory

of *Grossraumwirtschaft,* the economy of large spaces. The
U.S. and USSR had whole continents, Britain and France
had colonial empires; what was Germany to do? (Barraclough,
1976:87). Already during the thirties Germany had created a
separate trading bloc, a mark zone, to the east and south; in
1939, the proportion of imports coming from Germany was
65.5% in Bulgaria, 51% in Turkey, 48.4% in Hungary, 47.6%
in Yugoslavia, 39.2% in Romania (Milward, 1976: 403).
During the war, before defeat was imminent, the fruits of
rearmament were harvested; "the total contribution from the
French economy to the German amounted to one-third of
French national income in 1942 and almost one-half in 1943"
(Milward, 1976:404). In occupied Norway, extensive aluminum
manufacture was planned to supply the German aircraft
industry; the plan was based on permanent control over the
bauxite supply from Hungary, Croatia, and France. Milward
seems to me to miss the point when he stresses the economic
irrationality of the extermination policy after defeat was
clearly coming: "When in 1944 Germany faced extinction and
labour had become a scarce economic factor, the concentration
camps used labour at risibly low levels of productivity while
valuable resources were *increasingly* allocated to the slaughter
of all who were deemed of the wrong race" (1976:411; italics
in the original). By 1944 the Nazis were no longer "Germany"
but once again a movement.

Such is the trajectory of a movement called upon to break
the stalemated class struggle and get the German economy
moving again but marching to a somewhat different drummer.
What did they do? They aestheticized politics with spectacular
rallies. They attempted to neutralize and even coddle labor
with Munsterberg's industrial psychology and the beautification
of the plant. Their rearmament and public works policies
continued the concentration and rationalization of capital
such that the trends their ideology decried were accelerated
rather than reversed. They pioneered the administration of
consciousness and the reduction of the public sphere to
symbolism and propaganda (Rabinbach, 1976b). They expanded

externally in order to create "the only conditions under which the government thought it safe to increase the coercion and exploitation of labor, to depart from conservative principles of sound finance, and to intensify government control over business." "Collapse and chaos"—Hitler would not risk a falling standard of living—were the only alternatives to dynamic expansionism, so all solutions were temporary, hectic, hand-to-mouth affairs, increasingly barbaric improvisations around a brutal theme" (Mason, 1964, 1966).

What of the remainder of the core? Why did sects and movements emerge where they did? How were the regimes different from German fascism, even as they responded to the contraction in somewhat comparable ways? First, sects and movements. In France, many were launched but none could sail very far; the largest "an amorphous veterans association" called the Croix de Feu, the most serious the Parti Populaire Français. The standard comparison with Germany suggests that France neither suffered "national status deprivation," nor was its middle class so hurt by the depression, nor did its parliamentary system so lack legitimacy, nor was there serious ethnic rivalry; in short, no crisis of modernization (Payne, 1976). Could one not also (instead?) suggest that colonial profits, a relatively underpopulated countryside, and the slower growth of monopoly capital saved the French middle class?

In Belgium, middle-class Walloons gave considerable support to the Rex; two smaller fascist parties appeared in Flanders, one corporatist and conservative, the other anti-Semitic and pro-Nazi. In the Netherlands, Mussert's NSB—which, incidentally, had considerable strength in Indonesia—managed 4% of the vote in the 1937 elections. In England, Mosley's British Union of Fascists was increasingly influenced by Nazi ideology but "distinguished primarily by its impotence" (Payne, 1976). In the United States, finally, there was Father Coughlin and the KKK, widespread roundups and deportations of Mexican migrants, but no national organization of significance in spite of the admiration for Mussolini and Hitler in many circles. The critical point here seems to be that if no serious fascist movement had arisen in the twenties, the effects of the depression were not by themselves so severe as to generate more than echoes and imitations.

Comparisons among core *regimes* are more interesting. Recovery from the depression was the main policy problem, and with the uncertainties of the international economy, several mutually defeating alternatives were essayed. Kindleberger (1973) claims that the depression was so profound and prolonged because Britain was no longer able and the U.S. (for internal political reasons) unwilling to assume responsibility for the system as a whole. But his account does nothing to suggest that the United States was actually strong enough (nor the system as a whole rich enough) to take such leadership at least until 1936. Perhaps the major consequence of the war was to put the United States in a position of undisputed hegemony by weakening its competitors. The major difference between the fascist and liberal responses to the depression was in the treatment of organized labor and its parties, with recognition, co-optation, and mild income redistribution downward in the latter cases. But the similarities are notable: increases in industrial concentration, rearmament as the key to definitive recovery, widespread use of industrial psychology in factories (and recall as well the role of company goon squads in the United States even after the passage of the Wagner Act); special protection for agriculture, monumental architecture as part of public works programs, the definitive end of a political role for traditional conservatism, and the use of mass communications (fireside chats instead of Nuremberg rallies) to reassure and then in wartime to mobilize the civilian population. In the postwar core, the state hung onto its swollen proportions, as Claus Offe suggests, "interven[ing] in all spheres of society and at the same time retain[ing] a *relative* autonomy that avoids the *absolute* primacy of politics of fascism" (Rabinbach, 1974:153; italics in the original).

SEMI-PERIPHERY

The semi-periphery is the most controversial and slippery category in the world-systems model. Not merely a statistical artifact, there have not yet been established clear quantitative measures of the cutting points that demarcate semi-periphery from core at one end and periphery at the other. In my view it is crucial not to reify the notion, to keep in view the rising, stable, and falling semi-peripheral states in the context of a changing world economy, to recall the shifting advantages and disadvantages of size and distance as transport and communication technologies advance, and not to hypostatize, finally, the concept of industrialization. The semi-periphery is at once exploited and exploiting in the world production process, politically necessary if global class war is to be contained. In periods of contraction, some but not all semi-peripheral states can make great advances, partly at the expense of the declining core, partly at the expense of the weaker periphery (Wallerstein, 1976). In the period under review, Japan and the USSR did best, while Italy was hemmed in; Spain, Austria, and Czechoslovakia suffered, though Germany promoted certain industries in the latter two; Canada, South Africa, and Australia did quite well thanks to Commonwealth preferences and United States promotion; and Argentina was stuck. The basic characteristics of the semi-periphery in this period were existence of consumer goods industries (at least wage goods), adequate infrastructure, some heavy industrialization—but not much of a capital goods sector—some efficient but also some backward agriculture, and a medium-strength state.

To start with movements, in Spain the Falange was given a new lease on life by the Civil War but only insofar as it was transformed from a rather puny organization (0.44% of the vote in the 1936 elections) into Franco's official state party. Only weakly semi-peripheral to begin with, Spain suffered from an odd regional configuration which was the insurmountable legacy of Spanish failure in the "long" 16th century. The two most advanced areas, Catalonia and the Basque country, were also the most ethnically distinctive and separatist, while the historic integration of the agro-export South into the world economy had entrenched there a conservative, representative ruling class. The depression hurt: between 1928 and 1933 Spanish exports declined by two-thirds, and though the resulting popular pressure forced the end of the monarchy, the Second Republic was unable to produce either center-left or center-right coalitions that could reform or recover. Dim already, Spanish chances for an industrial breakthrough were wiped out in the Civil War, which Italian and German support decided for the insurgents. Fascist in repressive technique until the opposition was thoroughly crushed in the early forties, the Franco regime was basically conservative-authoritarian and as such a great disappointment both to Hitler and to the disillusioned native fascists (Linz, 1970).

The Austrian fascists found fertile soil among the déclassés, former professional soldiers of the Hapsburg monarchy and the insecure white-collar workers fearful of socialism, yet only with Anschluss did they come to power. Despite fascist pressure, the Dollfuss regime of the mid-thirties is best characterized as authoritarian.

Czechoslovakia, with its three major ethnic groups (53% Czech, 16% Slovak, 25% German), had three fascisms. The Czechs engendered some small sects whose nationalism was anti-German, and since German fascism presented far greater threats than the local left, the Czech sect disappeared entirely in 1938-1939. Slovak fascism was autonomist, Catholic in the popular sense, had important bases in the countryside, and is more properly peripheral; the fascism of backwardness, it came to power under the German occupation when Slovakia was made a separate state. The Germans in Czechoslovakia (three million of them, most in the Sudentenland, but also including 41% of the population of Prague) spawned fascism early, even before World War I. Like the Austrian party in the twenties, it was pan-German nationalist and closely linked to its German counterparts. In the depression, the obsolescent textile industry of German Bohemia suffered much more than the newer Czech iron and steel industry, just as they had in the German inflation of 1923-1924 when they were tied to the mark and the Czechs to the French franc. In 1938 the party became openly irredentist, won 88% of the German vote, and acted as the advance guard of the Nazi expansion (Sugar, 1971).

In Canada there arose the right-wing populist Social Credit Party, strongest in Alberta and British Columbia, and the anti-Semitic Union Nationale of Duplessis in Quebec. During the Duplessis machine's provincial rule, there were unpunished anti-Semitic riots in Montreal, Jehovah's Witnesses were locked up, the social sciences were curtailed at McGill University. In spite of rhetorical Québécois nationalism, there was concerted industrial growth under the aegis of English capital. In South Africa, the Nationalist Party of the Afrikaners (with much working-class support) echoed Nazi racism as it began its long rise against a backdrop of heavy industrialization; the party opposed South African participation in the war.

Let me talk about the fascist movement *and* regime in Italy, and then touch on Japan. Recall that the fascist sects made their starts in the immediate postwar period, with strong appeal to veterans, nationalist students, and to inhabitants of the border regions with Austria and Yugoslavia. But the key to the strength of Italian fascism—its surge as a mass movement in 1921—was its success in the countryside, particularly in the overpopulated, highly commercialized Po Valley, where the agrarian proletariat was heavily socialist and a serious threat to landowners' and middle peasants' authority and property rights. Mussolini and the urban fascists, with financial support from big industry and a social base among the petite bourgeoisie and professionals, were able to weld together a single party. In 1922 Mussolini moved to the right, identifying his party with what he saw as a general postwar counterrevolutionary trend (including the defeat of factory councils in Germany and Russia!), and stressing the need for order and authority. Throughout that year fascist *squadristi* kept up the pressure in the Northern cities, while unending parliamentary crisis left a continuing vacuum at the top; the largely mythic "March on Rome" left Mussolini at the head of a center-right ministry (Lyttelton, 1973, 1976).

As a regime, Italy's fascism was not nearly so "totalitarian" as Germany's: strong states in the core, not so strong in the semi-periphery, even with fascism. More independent centers of power remained, after the depression as well, and Mussolini was overthrown by the same sort of conservative groups which could not succeed against Hitler, even in 1944. The muzzling of labor politically went hand in hand with the promotion of industrialization and the rationalization of agriculture: land reclamation, public works, military contracts. The economy remained open in the twenties, growing rapidly to 1924, pausing for currency revaluation, and growing again until 1929; then after five years of depression and increased trade and import controls, the rapid growth resumed so that per capita income in 1936-1940 was 16.5% above that in 1921-1925. But as a percent of GNP industry only rose from 25% to 31% in all that time (Milward, 1976). And simultaneously, Italy was becoming a semi-peripheral client of Germany: the two primary exporters with the closest relations with Italy, Hungary, and Yugoslavia, redirected their trade toward Germany, leaving only Albania as an Italian preserve (Berend and Ranki, 1974). The political strength of France and Britain in the Middle East, and of Germany in Central and Eastern Europe left Italy nowhere to expand except Ethiopia; the fruits of that sorry conquest were not great, except perhaps for the Duce's propaganda output.

By comparison, Japan had a head start and a more open field. Short distances to Asian markets and low wages made Japanese exports highly competitive with those from Europe, especially in textiles. From 1913 to 1937, Japan's share of world manufactured exports rose from 2.5% to 7.5%; in the thirties, when more and more world trade was conducted bilaterally, the most spectacular shift took place in Japan's trade with the "yen bloc" of Korea, Formosa, Kwantung, and

Manchuria, where her exports rose from 25% to 55% between 1929 to 1938 and imports from 20% to 41% (Kindleberger, 1973:282).

The power constellation in Japan was dominated ultimately by the military, who had closer ties to the countryside and to anti-capitalist radicalism than was true of German fascism. The closest thing to a fascist movement was defeated in the abortive coup attempt in 1936, but that was only one step on the road to the consolidation of militarist hegemony in a context of undoing the tentative liberal openings of the twenties. Moore asserts that the industrialists had not been strong enough to make a "democratic breakthrough" in that period, but why should they have wanted to when the working class was their main potential ally and the state was already providing them with considerable support? Like Britain but without the Commonwealth, Japan was utterly dependent on trade, and when the core powers raised tariff walls in the wake of the depression, the Japanese has little choice but to seek a Greater East Asian Co-Prosperity Sphere under the slogan of Asia for the Asians—a Good Neighbor Policy with guns. In any case, their successes were numerous until they simultaneously ventured too far into China (where the United States hoped they would bog down) and then to protect their raw materials sources challenged the Anglo-Dutch-United States imperialist alliance in Southeast Asia. Pseudo-traditionalist and patriotic, with little trace of the technocratic mentality that was clearly an element in Nazism, Japan was fascist by alliance—and by imitation, e.g., the Imperial Rule Assistance Association (Wilson, 1968).

A brief comparison with the socialist semi-periphery will finish off this section. The USSR emerged from war, revolution, and civil war exhausted, devastated, and shorn of important western territories where nationalists, on the other hand, might have made things difficult for the fledgling Soviet state. For the USSR the choice was a stark one, though perhaps it was not stated so sharply: either develop military might through heavy industrialization, or face peripheralization. Japan had been in eastern Siberia until 1922; Germany would come crashing across the East European plains into Russia and the Ukraine in 1941. The period of world contraction (and the absence of any core power to the South?) gave the Soviets scarcely the time (and space) to defend themselves and to begin recovering the western territories as they tripled industrial production between 1929 and 1940. Let Polanyi tell the story of how "among the factors which forced upon her a decision [for 'socialism in one country']

> was the failure of the international system. By 1924 'War Communism' was a forgotten incident and Russia had reestablished a free domestic grain market, while maintaining state control of foreign trade and key industries. She was now bent on increasing her foreign trade, which depended mainly on exports of grain, timber, furs, and some other organic raw materials, the prices of which were slumping heavily in the course of the agrarian depression which preceded the general break in trade. Russia's inability to develop an export trade on favorable terms restricted her imports of machinery and hence the establishment of national industry: this, again, affected the terms of barter between town and countryside—the so-called 'scissors'— unfavorably, thus increasing the antagonism of the peasantry to the rule [sic] of the urban workers. In this way the disintegration of the world economy increased the strain on the makeshift solutions to the agrarian question in Russia, and hastened the coming of the kolkhoz. The failure of the traditional political system of Europe to provide safety and security worked in the same direction since it induced the need for armaments, thus enhancing the burdens of high-pressure industrialization. . . . Socialism in one country was brought about by the incapacity of market economy to provide a link between all countries; what appeared as Russian autarchy was merely the passing of capitalist internationalism. [1957:247-248]

So, rich in resources with a vast internal periphery to develop— as the Germans were enviously aware—the USSR squeezed the peasantry and coerced thousands of laborers in the camps, located much industry east of the Urals (in case of war?), crushed the independent plant level and political organization of the urban workers, and even purged the left wing of the socialist movement. No wonder, then, that Mussolini admiringly thought Stalin a fascist.

PERIPHERY

In the periphery there were numerous fascists sects, serious movements in Hungary, Romania, and perhaps Mexico, and several varieties of at least quasi-fascist regimes. These regimes borrowed elements from fascism—political style, or corporatist ideology, or openly racist practice, or anti-liberalism, to name a few—and can be reduced to three basic types. First, in those peripheral countries moving toward the semi-periphery there was import-substituting, developmentalist, urban populism: Brazil after 1942 and Argentina under Peron are the best examples. Second, there was conservative authoritarianism, mild where Jews and the left were negligible (Portugal, Bulgaria), more draconian where Jews were the primary "alien traders" and/or the left was stronger (Hungary, Romania, China). Third, there was ethnic integral nationalism; under the wartime German umbrella, it could be vicious in its attacks on rival ethnic groups (Slovakia, Croatia—more than half a million Serbs and Jews killed—and the Ukraine). In many colonial territories increased exploitation accompanied the fall in commodity prices, and with reduced demand, the export sectors sent labor back to the reserve areas often called "traditional." Perhaps the most fitting contrast with these fascist phenomena were the anti-imperialist populist nationalisms of Mexico, of the Indian Congress Party, of the democratic and/or socialist anti-colonial movements in Asia and Africa.

The Brazilian Integralistas and the Argentine ADUNA flourished in the mid-thirties but, lacking sufficient support within the army, neither was able to secure state power. Vargas's Estado Novo contained and repressed independent worker organization but introduced protective social legislation, and was primarily based on the "bureaucratic middle class and rural notables." As industrialization expanded and wartime U.S. demand for Brazilian primary exports grew,

Vargas shifted his base toward the industrialists and the urban workers (Hennessy, 1976). Argentina presents a case of mistimed developmentalism: the Peronist program of autarchic heavy industrialization coupled with economic penetration of Bolivia, Paraguay, and Chile did not take shape until the later forties when United States hegemony insured its failure. In spite of its anti-liberalism, Peronism was not fascism (*pace* Lipset), but it was too late. In addition it was also compromised with its working-class social base perhaps including Eva Peron's *descamisados*: necessary for Peron's continuing political power yet dependent on the state, these groups ate up too much of the treasure accumulated during the war in high wages and social benefits.

Of the more traditional conservative authoritarian regimes, little need be said. Corporatist Portugal under Salazar maintained a calm and neutral peripherality, with the regime based on the military and the bureaucracy. Salazar dissolved the only serious fascist sect after an abortive rising in 1934. The Bulgaria of Boris III (1935-1943) kept the lid on while carrying out the terms of the 1933 trade agreement with Germany by reorienting agricultural specialization toward oil-bearing crops, fodder, and animal products (Berend and Ranki, 1974:274).

Hungary and Romania are more complicated cases. Hungary, more industrial and with territorial claims arising from the aftermath of World War I, had a gentry-dominated regime under Admiral Horthy. It allied itself eventually with Germany and became preemptively more fascist. For it was threatened from below by the Arrow Cross, a strong fascist movement with considerable appeal to the peasantry and working class (especially the unskilled and unemployed) and with a solid base among sectors of the urban middle class and the gentry. During the war, "Magyar neoimperialism" had a brief resurgence, as the non-Magyars in the areas returned to Hungary in 1938-1941 were treated brutally, suffering along with the Jews from some of the most horrible anti-civilian excesses (Sugar, 1971). When Horthy tried prematurely to surrender to the Allies

(October 1944) the Germans deposed him, installed Szalasi's Arrow Cross in power, and brought on six months of warfare and a reign of terror. Despite its semi-peripheral industrial potential, Hungary was first treated as a peripheral element within the German *Grossraumwirtschaft* that included the Austro-Czech semi-periphery. (In 1937, Germany's per capita income was $340, Austria's $190, Czechoslovakia's $170, Hungary's $120, Romania's $81, Bulgaria's $75.) Germany had three aims in Hungary: "controlled cooperation" in agriculture, existing branches of industry under German control, and the prevention of new industrial development. This latter changed after mid-1941 with the changing requirements of the German military machine, even including aluminum and aircraft production, a form of "promotion" to the semi-periphery which ultimately "strengthened Hungary's position in relation to the other countries of Southeastern Europe" (Berend and Ranki, 1974, Chs. 11-13).

Romania experienced numerous fascist formations: the nationalistic and anti-Semitic National Christian party (a merger of two earlier organizations); Cordreanu's agrarian populist Iron Guard with its paramilitary Legion of the Archangel Michael; King Carol's monarcho-fascist regime—an attempt to prevent the Iron Guard from coming to power; and during the war, Antonescu's fascist military dictatorship which was achieved by crushing the Guard after briefly sharing power with it. Boundary shifts after World War I increased the nationality problems within this peripheral country, but especially with regard to the Jews. Jews were alien traders, commercial representatives of the despised and envied West, agents of absentee landlords, and also leading elements among the skilled socialist workers. Thus anti-Semitism *was* nationalism, and almost all interpreters agree that Romanian fascism was almost entirely autochthonous: by the barest of margins and only with German help did first King Carol and then Marshal Antonescu manage to keep the Iron Guard from power and hence to preserve the social regime of estate agriculture. The depression had to play a major role in the growth and strength of the Guard: Romania was very hard hit, so that from 1929 to 1934 cereals exports fell 42% in volume and 73% in generated earnings; even tripled oil exports generated slightly less income. Barter arrangements with Germany helped ease recovery but as with Hungary new specializations were demanded, here linseed and soy beans. Between 1937 and 1939 exports to Germany as a percent of total exports jumped from 19.1% to 43.1%, imports from 28.9% to 56.1%. (Again, this mirrored Hungary: 24.1% to 52.4% in exports; 26.2% to 52.5% in imports.) The new 1939 agreement gave Germany virtual monopoly control over Romanian foreign trade, confirmed the adjustment of Romanian agriculture to German demands, and resulted in the establishment of joint firms to exploit Romanian mineral resources (Vago, 1976; Berand and Ranki, 1974, Ch. 13). The Germans themselves thus had a clear interest in preventing the local native fascism with strong popular roots from interfering—whether by hooliganism or by land reform—in the intensified peripheralization of the Romanian economy.

Let me skip over the complicated tangle that was KMT China, a quasi-fascist regime that was basically the creature of the landlord class and the compradors, colonial-fascist, if you will, and move on briefly to the third type of peripheral fascism, the integral nationalism of Croatia (the People's Party of Hlinka), Slovakia (the Ustachi), and the Ukraine (the OUN). As ethnic movements in minority regions dominated by Serbs, Czechs, and Russians the first two had a brief chance to organize German-dominated independent states, the third for a time collaborated with the German occupation until it became clear that the Nazis aimed to reduce the Ukrainians to serfdom. The Slovakian party was anti-Czech, anti-Semitic, anti-communist, and clerical at the popular level (the Czechs were less enthusiastic Catholics); it took on more and more fascist characteristics after 1938. As a regime it had its own special courts and secret police, even concentration camps for opponents. Savage with the Jews, the Slovak state nonetheless suffered from typical peripheral weakness and was unable to prevent the organization of a strong underground that helped the Russian army liberate Slovakia from the Germans. In Yugoslavia there were whispers of fascist sects in the twenties and thirties but the conservative authoritarianism of King Alexander and the negative prestige of Italy kept them fairly insignificant until the late thirties, when German influence grew. Only the Croatian Ustachi was serious enough to be banned; heavily Catholic, anti-communist, anti-Semitic, anti-Serb, and middle class, its members included exiles in Germany, Italy, Hungary, and Bulgaria, and connections with the Macedonian separatists. They gained influence through the Croat Peasant Party, were encouraged by the break-up of Czechoslovakia, and came to power in 1941. As mentioned earlier, they killed over one-half million Serbs and Jews during their brief reign. All three territories—Croatia, Slovakia, and the Ukraine— played peripheral roles in the *Grossraumwirtschaft*; and all three show that a state need not be strong to be murderous (Sugar, 1971; Vago, 1976; Berend and Ranki, 1974).

CONCLUSION

In this overview of fascist phenomena, I have tried to sketch the way the world-systems perspective can order, if not fully interpret, the great transformations of the modern era: contraction in the global economy, hegemonic transition and power struggle in the core, opportunity and disaster in the semi-periphery, involution and conservatism in the periphery. A more detailed comparative analysis must await another occasion. Everywhere state intervention in the economy increased, through exchange controls and tariffs, reconstruction loans and direct investments, the repression or regulation of organized labor; but in the periphery it was as likely as not to be some foreign state that was doing the intervention. In the aftermath of World War I, fascist movements arose in a number of countries as an expression of the disappointed nationalism of some groups and the reactive class struggle of others. If World War I was

the war to end all wars, fascism was to be the struggle to end
the class struggle. In Germany, where fascist aims sufficiently
coincided with those of the conservative right and important
groupings of capital, the fascist breakthrough was achieved.
That breakthrough determined much of the rest—the rise of
more sects, movements, regimes. Meanwhile, it was the Great
Depression—its severity a function of the hegemonic transition—that made the German breakthrough possible, gave
"socialism in one country" its desperate character, exacerbated
the militarist expansionism of Japan, raised the ante for the
United States and the European core powers in Asia as well
as in the West. The Western working classes had achieved
considerable political strength in the previous period of
expansion, before World War I; but nationalism proved stronger
than socialism and before long they would suffer the effects
of national socialism as well as achieving the welfare state.

What of the present and the immediate future? Do the
fascistic regimes of today's semi-periphery foreshadow fascism in
the core, as Italy did Germany? If the present stagnation continues or worsens, as many predict, will fascism continue to
spread? Let me make some comparative observations.

First, accepting that the present stagnation is serious and
likely to grow worse, it will probably not be so cataclysmic
as that of the thirties, precisely because we are at the very
beginning rather than the end of a hegemonic transition within
the core. In more ways than one we are experiencing doldrums
comparable to the period after 1873, when British dominance
was giving way to haute finance under strong British influence.
That is what the Trilateral Commission, with its aim even
to integrate the USSR, is all about. But is Brezhnev the Bismarck
of the moment, looking to buy time with détente, to buy
technology with Western credits? That is what the debate
over Soviet intentions and capabilities is all about. "Are we
Financing the Hangman?" asked a right-wing columnist in
March 1977. The Chinese, we might note, *do* expect the USSR
to start a war within 20 or so years. But nuclear weapons
may mean that no one will risk a general conflagration.

Second, in the core and at the least the socialist semi-periphery, the state is much stronger relative to civil society than it was in the interwar years. Working-class gains from the pre-1970 boom are being eroded, but very slowly, while most of the suffering that is not shifted to the periphery is passed on to the dependent population: the elderly, the chronically or permanently unemployed, the institutionalized inmates, even the young, who are growing up with lower expectations. Opinion polling permits at least symbolic responsiveness to public anxieties, and where they were not before, electoral systems have tended toward the rather stable configuration of two- as opposed to multi-party situations. These features, plus the very heterogeneity of core societies, make radical mass movements extremely unlikely, whether from the left or the right. Tighter administration and increased repression à la Nixon, Brezhnev, or Gierek, are the probable government answers to the militant popular struggles that might arise from a serious depression. Meanwhile, the integration of women (and in the United States racial minorities) into high governmental and professional positions may well dampen fascist potential: fascist movements were heavily macho and in Northern Europe, of course, racist. And perhaps even the capitalist class learned from the earlier fascist experience that co-optation is preferable where at all possible. So in the core, despite some erosion of civil liberties and callous treatment of foreign workers, a fascist revival seems not on the horizon.

But in the periphery and capitalist semi-periphery, echoes, imitations, even recapitulations of fascist regimes seem destined to persist. The use of terror, torture, and/or near-starvation against workers, peasants, and their political organizations has increased considerably over the past 15 years, just about wherever the left has mounted a serious threat. These regimes and sometimes their paramilitary branches have arisen from *within* the state, notably the military and police branches, and with considerable tutelage from the United States. In South America, the semi-periphery is sorting itself out so that Brazil is moving up, Uruguay, Argentina, and Chile moving down, the former with a quasi-fascism of expansion (worked out in the Brazilian War College in the early sixties), the latter three with the fascism of peripheralization. Bolivia and Paraguay remain peripheral, the degree of threat from the left determining the extent of the repression. In South and Southeast Asia, in the Middle East, in Africa, and much of the rest of Latin America, where capitalists and state bureaucrats face threats but also see opportunities, we shall probably see more fascism than socialism before the 1980s are over. President Carter may smile on human rights, but the teeth of the world's policeman—its offspring, its clients—are biting around the globe.

REFERENCES

ANDERSON, P. (1976). Considerations on Western Marxism. London: New Left Books.
ARENDT, H. (1961). The origins of totalitarianism. Cleveland: World.
BARRACLOUGH, G. (1967). An introduction to contemporary history. Baltimore: Pelican.
BEREND, I.T., and RANKI, G. (1974). Economic development in east-central Europe in the 19th and 20th centuries. New York: Columbia University Press.
BRACHER, K.D. (1970). The German dictatorship. New York: Praeger.
——— (1976). "The role of Hitler: Perspectives of interpretation." pp. 211-225 in Laqueur (1976).
CARR, W. (1976). "National socialism—Foreign policy and wehrmacht." Pp. 151-178 in Laqueur (1976).
CARSTEN, F.L. (1976). "Interpretations of fascism." pp. 415-434 in Laqueur (1976).
CHIROT, D. (1977). Social change in the twentieth century. New York: Harcourt, Brace, Jovanovich.
DAHRENDORF, R. (1969). Society and democracy in Germany. Garden City: Anchor.
de FELICE, R. (1977). Interpretations of fascism. Cambridge: Harvard University Press.
DOBB, M. (1963). Studies in the development of capitalism. New York: International Publishers.
DOWD, D.F. (1955). "Economic stagnation in Europe in the interwar period." Journal of Economic History, 15(September):273-280.
GREGOR, A.J. (1974). The fascist persuasion in radical politics. Princeton: Princeton University Press.
HENNESSY, A. (1976). "Fascism and populism in Latin America." pp. 255-294 in Laqueur (1976).
KINDLEBERGER, C. (1973). The world in depression, 1929-1939. Berkeley: University of California Press.

KORNHAUSER, W. (1959). The politics of mass society. Glencoe, Ill.: Free Press.

LAQUEUR, W.Z. (ed., 1976). Fascism, A reader's guide. Berkeley: University of California Press.

LAQUEUR, W.Z., and MOSSE, G.L. (eds., 1966). International fascism, 1920-1945. New York: Harper and Row.

LEDEEN, M.A. (1972). Universal fascism: The theory and practice of the fascist international, 1928-1936. New York: Howard Fertig.

LINZ, J.J. (1970). "From Falange to Movimiento-Organización: The Spanish single party and the Franco Regime, 1936-1968." Pp. 128-202 in S.P. Huntington and C.H. Moore (eds.), Authoritarian politics in modern society. New York: Basic Books.

———— (1976). "Some notes toward a comparative study of fascism in sociological historical perspective." Pp. 3-121 in Laqueur (1976).

LINZ, J.J., and de MIGUEL, A. (1966). "Within-nation differences and comparisons: The eight Spains." Pp. 267-318 in R.L. Merritt and S. Rokkan (eds.), Comparing nations. New Haven: Yale University Press.

LIPSET, S.M. (1963). Political man. Garden City: Anchor.

LYTTELTON, A. (1973). The seizure of power: Fascism in Italy 1919-1929. New York: Scribner's.

———— (1976). "Italian fascism." Pp. 125-150 in Laqueur (1976).

MacDONALD, C.A. (1972). "Economic appeasement and the German 'moderates' 1937-1939." Past and Present, 56(August):105-135.

MASON, T.S. (1964). "Some origins of the Second World War." Past and Present, 29(December):57-87.

———— (1966). "Labour in the Third Reich." Past and Present, 33(April):112-141.

MILWARD, A.S. (1976). "Fascism and the economy." Pp. 379-412 in Laqueur (1976).

MOMMSEN, H. (1976). "National socialism—Continuity and change." Pp. 179-210 in Laqueur (1976).

MOORE, B., Jr. (1966). Social origins of democracy and dictatorship. Boston: Beacon.

PARSONS, T. (1954). Essays in sociological theory. Glencoe, Ill. Free Press.

PAYNE, S.G. (1976). "Fascism in Western Europe." Pp. 295-311 in Laqueur (1976).

POLANYI, K. (1957). The great transformation. Boston: Beacon.

POULANTZAS, N. (1974). Fascism and dictatorship. London: New Left Books.

RABINBACH, A.G. (1974). "Towards a Marxist theory of fascism and national socialism: A report on developments in West Germany." New German Critique, 3(fall):127-153.

———— (1976a). "Poulantzas and the problem of fascism." New German Critique, 8(spring):157-153.

———— (1976b). "The aesthetics of production in the Third Reich." Journal of Contemporary History, 11:43-74.

SARTI, R. (1970). "Mussolini and the Italian industrial leadership in the battle of the lira 1925-1927." Past and Present, 47(May):97-112.

SCHMITTER, P.C. (1974). "Still the century of corporatism?" Review of Politics, 36(January).

SCHOENBAUM, D. (1967). Hitler's social revolution. Garden City: Anchor.

STERNHILL, Z. (1976). "Fascist ideology." Pp. 315-376 in Laqueur (1976).

SUGAR, P.F. (ed., 1971). Native fascism in the successor states 1918-1945. Santa Barbara: ABC-Clio.

VAGO, B. (1976). "Fascism in Eastern Europe." Pp. 229-254 in Laqueur (1976).

WALLERSTEIN, I. (1974a). The modern world-system. New York: Academic Press.

——— (1974b). "The rise and future demise of the world capitalist system: Concepts for comparative analysis." Comparative Studies in Society and History, 16 (December):387-415.

——— (1976). "Semi-peripheral countries and the contemporary world crisis." Theory and Society, 3:461-483.

WATT, D.C. (1956). "The Anglo-German Naval Agreement of 1935." Journal of Modern History, 28(June):155-175.

WILSON, G.M. (1968). "A new look at the problem of 'Japanese fascism'." Comparative Studies in Society and History, 10:401-412.

PART 2

REVOLUTION AND THE WORLD SYSTEM

Chapter 4

REVOLUTIONS AND THE WORLD-HISTORICAL
DEVELOPMENT OF CAPITALISM

Theda Skocpol
Ellen Kay Trimberger

I

Before we launch into critical discussion, let us briefly underline some aspects of Marx's approach to revolutions[1] that are still compelling and which we want to recapitulate in our own approach. First, unlike many contemporary academic social scientists, Marx did not try to create a general theory of revolution relevant to all kinds of societies at all times. Instead he regarded revolutions as specific to certain historical circumstances and to certain types of societies. In accord with this mode of analysis, our arguments about revolutions apply specifically to agrarian states situated in disadvantaged positions within developing world capitalism. It seems to us that revolutions in advanced industrial capitalist or state-socialist societies would have different forms and occur in different ways.

Authors' Note: A version of this paper was first presented at the First Annual Conference on the Political Economy of the World System at American University on March 31, 1977. Subsequently a fuller version—substantially the one published here, with only minor additional revisions—was presented at the session on the "Sociology of the World System" at the 72nd Annual Meeting of the American Sociological Association, Chicago, September 5, 1977.

Second, Marx developed a social-structural theory of revolutions which argued that organized and conscious movements for revolutionary change succeed only where and when there is an objectively revolutionary situation, due to contradictions in the larger societal structure and historical situation: thus, Marx's oft-quoted saying that men make their own history, but not in circumstances of their own choosing and not just as they please. We have a different conception from Marx about what creates objectively revolutionary crises, but our analysis, like his, hinges on discerning how revolutionary situations arise out of structural relations and historical processes outside of the deliberate control of acting groups.

Third, Marx made class domination central to his conception of social order, and class conflict a defining feature of revolution, and we retain such concerns. In her work on revolutions from above, Trimberger defines revolution as any extralegal takeover of the state apparatus that destroys the political and economic power of that class which controlled the dominant means of production under the old regime. And in her work on mass-based social revolutions from below, Skocpol defined this particular type of revolution as a sudden, basic transformation of a society's political and socioeconomic (including class) structure, accompanied and in part effectuated through class upheavals from below.

Taking off from these continuities with Marx's approach to revolutions, we can now identify various points at which Marx's original theory[2] of revolutions stands in need of revision when juxtaposed to historical revolutions from above and below as we understand them. We shall discuss in turn issues about causes, processes, and outcomes of revolutions.

Karl Marx's theory of revolutions was elegant, powerful, and politically relevant because it linked the causes and consequences of revolutions directly to the historical emergence and transcendence of capitalism. Nevertheless events and scholarship since Marx's time show that there is a need for revised ways of understanding revolutions in relation to the world-historical development of capitalism. In the spirit of furthering theoretical efforts to this end, we propose to do two things in this short paper. First, we shall identify the essential elements of Marx's original theory of revolutions and indicate some important ways in which his ideas fail to square with the actual patterns of revolutions as they have occurred historically. Then we shall suggest some alternative analytic emphases that must in our opinion underlie explanations of major types of historical revolutions and efforts to situate them in relation to the development of capitalism. In doing these things, we shall draw especially upon our own comparative historical investigations of social revolutions in France, Russia, and China (Skocpol 1976a, 1976b, forthcoming) and of bureaucratic revolutions from above in Japan and Turkey (Trimberger 1972, 1977a, 1977b), as well as upon the work of scholars such as Immanuel Wallerstein (1974a, 1974c), Otto Hintze (1929), and Daniel Chirot (1977) who have explored transnational aspects of capitalism as a world system.

CAUSES

Marx held that a revolutionary situation occurs when an existing mode of production reaches the limits of its contradictions. The decisive contradictions are *economic* contradictions that develop between the social forces and the social relations of production. In turn, intensifying class conflict is generated between the existing dominant class and the rising revolutionary class. Thus Marx theorized that revolutionary contradictions are internally generated within a society. What is more, his perspective strongly suggested that revolutions should occur first in the most economically advanced social formations of a given mode of production.

Actual historical revolutions, though, have not conformed to Marx's theoretical expectations. From the French Revolution on, they have occurred in predominantly agrarian countries where capitalist relations of production were only barely or moderately developed. In every instance, political-military pressures from more economically advanced countries abroad have been crucial in contributing to the outbreak of revolution. And, most important, the objective contradictions within the old regimes that explain the emergence of revolutionary situations have not been primarily economic. Rather they have been *political* contradictions centered in the structure and situation of states caught in cross-pressures between, on the one hand, military competitors on the international scene and, on the other hand, the constraints of the existing domestic economy and (in some cases) resistance by internal politically powerful class forces to efforts by the state to mobilize resources to meet international competition. Thus, to mention some examples: the Japanese Meiji Restoration (a bureaucratic revolution from above) occurred because the Tokugawa state (which was already highly bureaucratic) came under severe and novel pressures from imperialist capitalist Western powers; the French and Chinese revolutions broke out because the Bourbon and Manchu regimes were caught in contradictions between pressures from economically more developed foreign states and resistance from dominant class forces at home; and the Russian Revolution broke out because the Tsarist bureaucracy and military dissolved under the impact of World War I upon economically backward Russia.

PROCESSES

Marx theorized that, given a revolutionary situation, revolutions are fundamentally accomplished through class struggles led by that class which emerges within the womb of the old mode of production and becomes central to the new, post-revolutionary mode of production. Historically only two classes play this leading revolutionary role. In bourgeois revolutions, a capitalist class that has grown up within feudalism plays the leading role in the revolutionary class conflicts by which feudal relations of production are overthrown and capitalism established instead. In socialist revolutions the proletariat plays the leading role. In either type of revolution, the hegemonic revolutionary class may have allies, such as the peasantry. But such subordinate, allied classes are not capable of becoming nationally organized and self-conscious classes-for-themselves, and, consequently, they do not control the revolutionary process or outcomes in their own interests, as does the leading revolutionary class.

On the basis of the historical record, two major sets of reservations need to be registered about these ideas of Marx. One point has to do with the relative contributions of class forces and political leaderships to the accomplishment of revolutions. Some revolutions—i.e., revolutions from above—which have had outcomes and consequences that seem quite revolutionary from a Marxist perspective, have not actually been made by class forces or through class struggles; instead, bureaucratic-military political elites have reorganized states and used state power to effect socioeconomic structural transformations. Other revolutions (specifically social revolutions such as the French, Russian, Chinese, Mexican, Vietnamese, and Angolan) *have* been effected in part through class struggles. But, here too, political leadership groups have played very central roles.[3] How, for example, could the processes and outcomes of the Russian, Chinese, and Vietnamese revolutions be understood without attention to the contribution of Leninist-Communist parties, or the French Revolution without attention to the role of the Jacobins and Napoleon? In short, during revolutions political conflicts generate leadership groups from the ranks of educated strata oriented to state service—and this happens whether or not basic class struggles are involved. Moreover, it does not make sense to try to reduce the contribution of revolutionary parties or bureaucratic-military elites to that of merely representing and acting along with class forces, since these specifically political forces are uniquely responsible for consolidating revolutions by establishing new state organizations.

The second point to be made in reaction to Marx's views on the processes of revolutions has to do with which classes actually are central to revolutions. Contrary to Marx's argument that the struggles of the bourgeoisie or proletariat would have the most impact, it has actually been the peasantry (struggling against formerly dominant landed classes (and/or colonial or neo-colonial regimes) that has done the most—specifically in social revolutions from below—to undermine the class and political structures of old regimes and clear the way for the consolidation of revolutionary states on a new socioeconomic and political basis.[4] In our view, there never has been an instance of class-conscious capitalist bourgeoisie playing the leading political role in a revolution (though of course some revolutions have contributed in their outcomes to the further or future growth of captialism and bourgeois class dominance). As for the proletariat, it indeed contributed crucially to the accomplishment of the Russian Revolution in particular, but, arguably, it was not as decisive in destroying the Old Regime as the peasantry, and its class interests were compromised just as thoroughly, and even sooner, than the peasantry's as the Bolsheviks consolidated party-state power after 1917.

OUTCOMES

Finally, we arrive at the issue of what revolutions immediately accomplish once they have successfully occurred. Marx held that revolutions mark the transition from one mode of production to another, that they so transform socioeconomic conditions as to create conditions newly appropriate for further rapid economic development. Superstructural transformations of ideology and the state also occur, but these were seen by Marx as parallel to and reinforcing the fundamental socioeconomic changes.

Yet, historically, revolutions have changed state structures as much or more than they have changed class relations of production and surplus appropriation. In all of the cases of revolution from above and below that we studied, state structures became suddenly much more centralized and bureaucratic. And Third World revolutions since World War II have broken or weakened the bonds of colonial or neo-colonial dependency, above all by creating truly sovereign and, in some cases, mass-mobilizing, national governments (see Dunn, 1972; Chaliand, 1977). Equally important, the effects that revolutions have had upon the subsequent economic development of the nations they have transformed have been traceable not only to the changes in class structures but also to the *changes in state structures and functions* that the revolutions accomplished. As Immanuel Wallerstein (1971:364) has very aptly argued, "development [i.e., national economic development] does require a 'breakthrough.' But it is a political breakthrough that in turn makes possible the far more gradual economic process."

II

If Marx's original elegant theory is no longer entirely adequate, then how can we make sense in new ways of revolutions in relation to the development of capitalism? Obviously we are not going to be able to provide complete answers here. But we can propose three analytic principles that we have found especially useful in our own efforts to explain revolutions from above and below in agrarian states situated within developing world capitalism. These are: (1) a nonreductionist conception of states; (2) social-structural analyses of the situation of the peasantry within the old and new regimes (and for cases of social revolution from below, in relation to the organized revolutionary leadership); and (3) a focus on international military competition among states within the historically developing world capitalist economy. Let us elaborate each point in turn.

THE STATE

We believe that states should be viewed theoretically as conditioned by, but not entirely reducible in their structure or functioning to, economic and/or class interests or structures. States are neither mere instruments of dominant class forces nor structures simply shaped by objective economic constraints. Rather, states are fundamentally administrative and military organizations that extract resources from society and deploy them to maintain order at home and to compete against other states abroad. Consequently, while it is always true that states are greatly constrained by economic conditions and partly shaped and influenced by class forces, nevertheless state structures and activities also have an underlying integrity and a logic of their own, and these are keyed to the dynamics of international military rivalries and to the geopolitical as well as world-economic circumstances in which given states find themselves.

This conception of states[5] helps to make sense of certain of the facts about the causes of revolutions that seemed so jarring when placed in juxtaposition with Marx's original notions. For if states are coercive organizations not reducible to class structures, then it makes sense that processes that serve to undermine state strength should be crucial in bringing about revolutions from below, while revolutions from above are based upon political reorganization within a state that is already strong and autonomous over against class forces. In all of the five countries that we have studied most intensively— France, Russia, China, Japan, and Turkey—there were, prior to the revolutions, relatively centralized and partially bureau-cratic monarchical states, none of which had been incorporated into a colonial empire. As they came under pressure in a capitalist world, these states had the capacity to try to mobilize national resources to stave off foreign domination—something that occurred through revolution from above in Japan and Turkey, whereas the old regimes broke down completely in France, Russia, China, clearing the way for revolutions from below. Thus, Trimberger has demonstrated how in Japan the separation of samurai bureaucrats from control over the means of production and the absence of a consolidated landed class able to exert political influence permitted military bureaucrats to undertake, under foreign pressure, a revolution from above without mass participation that destroyed the traditional aristocracy and polity and established a modern state that fostered capitalist development. With more difficulty and less success, a similar process took place in Turkey. And Skocpol has shown how in Bourbon France and Imperial China politically powerful landed classes were able to limit the autonomy of civil and military state bureaucrats, undermining the effectiveness of their attempts at modernizing reforms and causing the disintegration of centralized repressive controls over the lower classes. In Russia, the landed nobility was much less politically powerful vis-à-vis reforming state authorities, but the agrarian class structure nevertheless limited Russia's ability to prepare for the exigencies of modern warfare so that the Tsarist state was overwhelmed and destroyed in World War I. The theoretically relevant point that applies to all of these cases regardless of the various patterns is that if one treats states theoretically as potentially autonomous, even vis-à-vis the existing class structure and dominant class, then one can explore the dynamic *interactions* between state organizations and dominant class interests. In situations of intense foreign politicomilitary pressure, these interactions can become contradictory and lead either to state action against dominant class interests or to dominant class forces acting in ways that undermine the state. Thus the nonreductionist theoretical approach to the state helps make sense of the specifically political crises that launch revolutions.

This conception of the state also helps to render understandable those aspects of the processes and outcomes of revolutions that Marx's class conflict theory of revolutions seemed to downplay or ignore. Revolutions are not consolidated until new or transformed state administrative and coercive organizations are securely established in the place of the old regime. Consequently, it makes sense that political leaderships— parties or bureaucratic/military cliques—that act to consolidate revolutionized state organizations should play a central role in revolutionary processes. And if states are extractive organizations that can deploy resources to some extent independently of existing class interests, then it makes sense that revolutions create the *potentials* for breakthroughs in national economic development in large part by giving rise to more powerful, centralized, and autonomous state organizations. This was true for all of the revolutions from above and below that we studied, although the potential for state-guided or initiated national economic development was more thoroughly realized in Japan, Russia, and China than it was in France and Turkey. For the actual realization of the revolution-created potential depends upon the international and world-historical economic constraints and opportunities specific to each case after the revolution. (On this point see also Eckstein, 1975a, 1975b.)

THE SITUATION OF THE PEASANTRY

In addition to looking at states as relatively autonomous and in dynamic interrelation with dominant classes, one should also pay careful attention to the situation of the peasantry in relation to the state and dominant class. Historically, mass-based social revolutions from below have successfully occurred only if the breakdown of old-regime state organizations has happened in an agrarian sociopolitical context where peasants, as the majority producing class, possess (or obtain) sufficient local economic and political autonomy to revolt against landlords. Such results occurred successfully in the French, Russian, and Chinese revolutions alike. By contrast (as Skocpol has argued), the German Revolution of 1848-1850 was condemned to failure by the lack of sociopolitical conditions conducive to peasant rebellion east of the Elbe. And it was certainly an important condition for revolutions *from above* in Japan and Turkey that peasants in those countries remained immured within traditional structures not conducive to widespread revolts from below against landlords.

What is more, the varying outcomes of successful social revolutions are significantly affected by the specific way in which the peasantry becomes involved in the overall revolutionary process, and by the nature of its relationship to the state organizations of the new regime. For, although Marx was mistaken to slight the revolutionary potential of the peasantry, he was not wrong in arguing that the peasantry is incapable of becoming a nationally self-organized class for itself. Peasants always end up being mobilized into revolutionary organizations and/or states. And the exact way in which this happens—whether, for example, by persuasion during the revolutionary process as in China and Vietnam, or by coercion after the initial consolidation of revolutionary state power, as in Russia—makes a big difference for the socioeconomic and political character of the revolutionary outcome. (Skocpol, 1976b, develops this argument at length for Russia and China in particular.)

THE INTERNATIONAL STATE SYSTEM

Finally we arrive at an analytic emphasis that can help make sense of the entire context within which the causes and outcomes of revolutions have been shaped and their consequences determined. In its theoretical essentials, this point has two parts: (a) capital should be conceived not only as a mode of production based upon a relationship between wage labor and accumulating capital, but also as a world economy with various zones that are interdependent and unequal (Wallerstein, 1974a, 1974c); and (b) capitalism from its inception has developed within, around, and through a framework of "multiple political sovereignties"—that is, the system of states that originally emerged from European feudalism (see Anderson, 1974; Tilly, 1975) and then expanded through the incorporation of preexisting imperial states, and through colonization followed eventually by decolonization, to cover the entire globe as a system of nations. We must emphasize that, in our view, this changing international system of states was not originally created by capitalism, and throughout modern world capitalist history represents an analytically autonomous level of transnational reality, *interdependent* in its structure and dynamics with the world economy, but not reducible to it. Indeed, just as capitalist economic development has spurred transformations of states and the international states system, so have these "acted back" upon the course of capital accumulation within nations and upon a world scale (see Hintze, 1929).

The significance of international military competition for helping to cause the revolutions from above and below that we have studied has been amply alluded to in our discussion of the state. Similarly John Dunn's studies (1972, 1975) of contemporary revolutions have led him to argue (1975:17) that "the great bulk of revolutionary success in the twentieth century has been intimately related to one or other of two very undomestic processes: world war and decolonization," both developments within the international state system of world capitalism.

The analysis of capitalism as a world system and of revolution as generated by state competition and state formation within this system also provides a framework from which to interpret the results of revolutions, and helps us to understand why there has been continual disillusionment when revolutionary outcomes failed to mesh with ideological claims. Although there have been important variations in the state structures that have emerged from revolutions, all revolutions during the evolution of world capitalism have given rise to more bureaucratized and centralized states, in part because of the need to cope with precisely those international pressures that helped to create the revolutionary crises in the first place. It is not just revolutions from above, but all revolutions that have become "bureaucratic revolutions"—in the specific sense of creating larger, more centralized, and more bureaucratized state organizations than existed under the old regimes (see, e.g., Chaliand, 1977). Revolutionary leaders have sought to enhance national standing and have seen the state apparatus as the most important tool to achieve this, especially where the state could be used to guide or undertake national industrialization. International pressures have been more effective in determining the outcomes of revolutions than intranational pressures for equality, participation, and decentralization. Even in China, where organized interests have fought for more equality and participation, the vulnerable international situation has always encouraged centralization and bureaucracy.

How are we, finally, to reason about the consequences of revolutions for the development of capitalism and its eventual transformation into socialism? For Marx, this problem could be straightforwardly handled: some revolutions (i.e., bourgeois revolutions) established capitalism, while others (i.e., socialist revolutions) abolished capitalism and created the conditions for the rapid emergence of communism. Marx's "mode of production" was at least implicitly identified with the socio-economic arrangement of a nation-state unit, and the major types of revolutions—bourgeois and socialist—were seen as succeeding each other as given nations developed through major stages from feudalism to capitalism to socialism. Subsequently, Lenin and Trotsky stressed the idea that the capitalist stage (and bourgeois revolution) could be in a sense compressed or skipped over if the proletariat rather than the bourgeoisie took the leading role in a backward country among a set of neighbor countries where revolutions would probably occur roughly simultaneously.

But actual revolutions have not readily conformed to the types and sequences originally projected by Marx or his successors. Certainly no country had had two successive revolutions, one bourgeois and the other socialist, and even revolutions that bear certain superficial resemblances to the "bourgeois" and "socialist" types do not really fit. Revolutions from above and below that have functioned to further bourgeois-capitalist development have not been "made by" class conscious bourgeoisies, and they have in fact furthered capitalist economic development precisely because they did not establish bourgeois class political hegemony in the sense of direct political rule by capitalists. As for "socialist revolutions," there have been revolutions made in part through class revolts from below that have culminated in the abolition of private property and the bourgeois class. Yet these have occurred in "backward" agrarian countries, and not solely or primarily through proletarian class action. The outcomes of these revolutions can be described as "state socialist" in the sense that party-states have taken direct control of national economies. Yet these regimes act, so to speak, in the place of the bourgeoisie to promote national industrialization and do not conform to (or converge upon) Marx's original vision of socialism or communism.

From the perspective that capitalism is transnational in scope, we see why Marx's original typology of revolutions cannot hold. Since revolutions have occurred only in specific countries within the capitalist world economy and the international state system, and at particular times in their world-historical development, it follows that no single revolution could possibly either fully establish capitalism or entirely overcome capitalism and establish socialism. Yet some theorists of the "world capitalist system" have taken a position on the consequences of revolutions that we find equally inadequate. For example, Immanuel Wallerstein has argued in places (e.g., 1974b, 1974c) that the occurrence of national revolutions which abolish capitalist private property in favor of state ownership and control of the means of production has not altered the basic economic structure and dynamics of the world capitalist system. We agree with Wallerstein that state ownership is not socialism, and that no alternative world socialist economy has yet been created. But one can agree with these conclusions while still maintaining that state-socialist revolutions such as the Russian and Chinese have made a real difference for world capitalism because they have culminated in regimes that place unusual and/or extreme restrictions on flows of international trade and private capital investment. To be sure, these restrictions are not absolute and, of course, they vary from one state-socialist country to another. But surely it matters for the structure, dynamics, and longevity of the world capitalist system that, for example in China, a state-socialist revolution occurred rather than a military coup culminating (as in Brazil) in a regime willing to collaborate intimately with foreign investors and willing to promote indus-trialization for export rather than for furthering more equal internal consumption. We agree with Daniel Chirot (1977: 232-233), who argues that even if "no unified communist international system exists, this does not lessen the long-range revolutionary threat to the system posed by the communist powers" since "as long as the main goal of [communist] revolu-tionaries . . . is closure to capitalist influence, the presence of a complete new alternative system is not necessary."

In the final analysis, though, we must always keep in mind that even if revolutions of some types—such as state socialist ones—do, relatively speaking, disrupt world capitalism (i.e., more than either nonrevolutions or nonstate socialist revolu-tions) this does not mean that they simultaneously build socialism. To do this they must *also* promote sociopolitical equality within and between nations. Both the capitalist world economy and the international state system have pressured reovlutionized countries in ways that make such more equali-tarian patterns difficult to achieve or sustain. Still, some revolutions have done better than others, and different inter-national circumstances provide only part of the reasons why. World systems analyses must be supplemented by comparative-historical studies of intranational structures and struggles. The specific societal configurations of state, economic, and class forces make a great difference in structuring the type of revolutionary outbreak and its consequences for both national and world-capitalist development. Undoubtedly, the equalitarian tendencies of the "state socialist" revolutions of China and Cuba, for example, have been constrained and limited by the necessities of competition and survival in a capitalist world. Nevertheless the internal class and political struggles that gave rise to those equalitarian tendencies in China and Cuba did make a difference compared to other state socialist revolutions (such as Russia) and compared to other revolutions that did not abolish private property. It was Marx himself who originally made the analysis of such struggles central to our understanding of revolutions. In this, he still has the last word.

NOTES

1. Our understanding of Marx's theory of revolutions is synthesized from wide reading in his writings, and we will not give references each time we discuss his views. Important texts for understanding Marx on revolutions include: "The Communist Manifesto," "The German Ideology," Preface to "A Contribution to the Critique of Political Economy," "The Eighteenth Brumaire of Louis Bonaparte" and "The Class Struggles in France." All of these are widely reprinted.

2. In this paper we are deliberately *not* exploring all of the changing emphases to be found in writings on revolution by Marxists since Marx. Nor are we exploring the many nuances to be found in Marx's own writings. Our purpose is to highlight crucial issues for further theorizing about revolutions. Since Marx's ideas are relatively widely known (and, in our view, still the most powerful ideas available about revolutions), we are using the rhetorical device of juxtaposing our arguments and sense of the historical evidence to the central thrust of Marx's theory.

3. This is suggested not only by our own work, but also by Wolf (1969, "Conclusion"), Dunn (1972), and Chaliand (1977).

4. Again, beyond our work, see Moore (1966), Wolf (1969), and Chaliand (1977).

5. Our argument about states resonates closely with Hintze (1906) and Tilly (1975) and it extends recent tendencies within Marxist scholarship (e.g., Poulantzas, 1973; Anderson, 1974; Block, 1977) to view state organizations and their "managers" as capable of independent initiatives vis-à-vis dominant classes. For a general survey of recent Marxist ideas on the state, see Gold, Lo, and Wright (1975).

REFERENCES

ANDERSON, P. (1974). Lineages of the absolutist state. London: New Left Books.
BLOCK, F. (1977). "The ruling class does not rule: Notes on the Marxist theory of the state." Socialist Revolution, 7(May-June):6-28.

CHALIAND, G. (1977). Revolution in the Third World: Myths and prospects. New York: Viking.

CHIROT, D. (1977). Social change in the twentieth century. New York: Harcourt, Brace, Jovanovich.

DUNN, J. (1972). Modern revolutions. New York and London: Cambridge University Press.

—— (1975). The success and failure of modern revolutions. Paper presented at the Workshop on the Sources of Radicalism and the Revolutionary Process, Research Institute on International Change, Columbia University, May 7.

ECKSTEIN, S. (1975a). "How economically consequential are revolutions?: A comparison of Mexico and Bolivia." Paper presented at the 70th Annual Meeting of the American Sociological Association, August 27.

—— (1975b). The impact of revolution: A comparative analysis of Mexico and Bolivia. Beverly Hills, Calif.: Sage.

GOLD, D., LO, C. and WRIGHT, E. (1975). "Recent developments in Marxist theories of the capitalist state." Monthly Review, (October):29-43; (November):36-51.

HINTZE, O. (1906). "Military organization and the organization of the state." Pp. 178-215 in F. Gilbert (ed.), The historical essays of Otto Hintze. new York: Oxford University Press.

—— (1929). "Economics and politics in the age of modern capitalilsm." Pp. 422-452 in F. Gilbert (ed.), The historical essays of Otto Hintze. New York: Oxford University Press.

MOORE, B., Jr. (1966). Social origins of dictatorship and democracy. Boston: Beacon.

POULANTZAS, N. (1973). Political power and social classes. London: New Left Books.

SKOCPOL, T. (1976a). "France, Russia, China: A structural analysis of social revolutions." Comparative Studies in Society and History, 18(April):175-210.

—— (1976b). "Old regime legacies and communist revolutions in Russia and China." Social Forces, 55(December):284-315.

—— (forthcoming). States and social revolutions in France, Russia, and China. New York and London: Cambridge University Press.

TILLY, C. (ed., 1975). The formation of national states in Western Europe. Princeton, N.J.: Princeton University Press.

TRIMBERGER, E.K. (1972). "A theory of elite revolutions." Studies in Comparative International Development, 7(fall):191-207.

—— (1977a). "State power and modes of production: Implications of the Japanese transition to capitalism." Insurgent Sociologist, 7(spring):85-98.

—— (1977b). Revolution from above: Military bureaucrats and modernization in Japan, Turkey, Egypt, and Peru. New Brunswick, N.J.: Trans-action Books.

WALLERSTEIN, I. (1971). "The state and social transformation: Will and possibility." Politics and Society, 1(May):359-364.

—— (1974a). The modern world-system: Capitalist agriculture and the origins of the European world-economy in the sixteenth century. New York: Academic Press.

—— (1974b). "Dependence in an interdependent world: The limited possibilities of transformation within the capitalist world economy." African Studies Review, 17(April):1-25.

———— (1974c). "The rise and future demise of the world capitalist system: Concepts for comparative analysis." Comparative Studies in Society and History, 16(September): 387-415.

WOLF, E. (1969). Peasant wars of the twentieth century. New York: Harper and Row.

Chapter 5

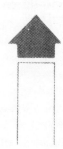

STATE CAPITALISM AND COUNTERREVOLUTION
IN THE MIDDLE EAST: A THESIS

Samih K. Farsoun
Walter F. Carroll

State-capitalism, while exhibiting many of the common external features of socialist development, is in reality the imposition of new forms on old structures, leading to a socio-economic impasse in which the older "structures" increasingly inform the newer forms.

The three principle contradictions of the state-capitalist society revolve around the conflict between dependence on advanced technology/marginalization of labor, between industrial expansion/modernization, between bureaucratic appropriation/exploitation of productive sectors. [*Petras, 1976a:22, 30*]

Two topics relatively neglected in American social science are the Middle East as an area of inquiry and the study of counterrevolution. Few American sociologists address themselves to the Middle East. In many disciplines, Orientalists still hold sway or modernization theorists muddle understanding.

In regard to the second topic, the study of revolution should, but too often does not, illuminate counterrevolution. This paper is an exploratory effort in both areas.

The civil war in Lebanon was ended by the Syrian army with the blessing of Egypt and Saudi Arabia. The Syrian army contained the Palestinian guerrillas and the Lebanese left while allying itself with the Lebanese right. This took place with the tacit agreement and coordination of the United States and Israel. The end of the civil war in Lebanon brought about a modicum of stability in the region, a necessary condition for political settlement of the Middle East conflict. These developments raise the following questions: Why have governments that previously supported the Palestinians reversed their roles? Why have governments which originated as anti-imperialist national liberation movements now entered into open collaboration with the United States? Of course, there are many corollary questions.

While we do not pretend to present full answers to these questions in this paper, we do intend to indicate the direction in which inquiry might fruitfully move, the kinds of data necessary to provide the answers, and a thesis which could organize the known data.

The rise of counterrevolution in the Middle East points up the weakness of the whole study of counterrevolution. There is, of course, Charles Tilly's classic study, *The Vendée* (1964), and his recent work which is promising. Arno Mayer's *Dynamics of Counterrevolution in Europe, 1870-1956* (1971) is insightful but is explicitly limited to Europe, the capitalist core, and does not deal with the periphery. He does make a point, however, which leads us in the proper direction:

> Counterrevolution is the product of a constellation of world history and not of localized national aberrations. [Mayer, 1971]

A world historical perspective is necessary. This need not mean adoption of a particular "political economy of the world-system" approach. The world-economy is not the only unit of analysis. The transnational perspective is a contextual variable in an analysis within which we situate national and regional levels of analysis. This avoids some of the problems of the world-system approach. As Colin Leys (1977) notes:

> It would be better to envisage the necessary development of a historical materialist context for future theory by way of *successive approximations* arising out of studies of historical situations specific enough for the study to be related in a very explicit way to the contemporary class struggles within them.

Thus, we attempt to link specific conjunctures and the processes of class struggle within them.

The rise, dynamics, and demise of Arab state-capitalist regimes must be seen in the context of national, regional, and world social, economic, and political forces. The key to understanding contemporary counterrevolution in the Arab periphery is related to the rise and destiny of state-capitalism as a specific mode of production with external linkages and internal contradictions. To anticipate the argument briefly, it is the resolution of these contradictions which determines the anti-imperialist or counterrevolutionary character of state-capitalism. but in the Arab periphery sources of the contradictions of both dependent neocolonial capitalism and state-capitalism are both the national and class questions. The absolutely crucial point is that these two questions are indissolubly linked and cannot be understood in isolation from each other (see Welty and Bowman, forthcoming).

THE RISE OF STATE CAPITALISM
AND ANTI-IMPERIALISM

Since World War I the Arab world has been characterized by a dramatic struggle of national liberation from Western imperialism and Zionist settler-colonialism. Because of the creation of Israel and the destruction of Palestine, the national question developed as the dominant and manifest contradiction in the region. Indeed, in the countries of the Arab east particularly, the class question became interlocked with the national question and was expressed in struggles initially against British and French colonialism and, after World War II, against American imperialism, all in alliance with Zionism and Israel.

The discredited ruling classes in the aftermath of the 1948 Palestine War—landlord, mercantile, and compradore bourgeoisie—lost control in several Arab countries of the state apparati to petite bourgeois "intermediary strata" as Petras (1976a,b) refers to them.

> the very origins of the(se) regime(s) are based on social and political "stalemate": when internal conflicts, mass pressure and imperial domination undermine the rule of the traditional landed and commercial strata and when the mobilized working and peasant classes, for lack of a revolutionary party, political consciousness, and/or revolutionary leadership are incapable of taking power, the military may appear on the scene as the "arbiter" of society. Through its control over the state apparatus it attempts to "mediate" between the masses and the national bourgeoisie. [1976b:439-440]

Taking power via a coup d'état, these "intermediary strata"— military-bureaucratic—justify their takeover of the state apparatus to the mobilized but unorganized masses by promising to resolve the crisis of the interlocked national and socioeconomic questions. These strata were able to project and propagate their own class interest as *the national* interest, and their own development project as the correct means for resolving *the national* socioeconomic crisis. Thus, they captured the leadership of the masses in the struggle for national liberation. This has been the popular basis of the class alliance in given states and on a pan-Arab level which fed Nasserism and Baathism. Both Nasserism and Baathism, which call for pan-Arab unity, freedom from foreign control, and "socialism" in that order, were the ideology of the Arab military-bureaucratic "intermediary strata" in their formative years after World War II and during their heyday into the mid-1960s. But this political, economic, and sociocultural liberation from foreign domination although couched in socialist rhetoric was nevertheless a project "whose conception . . . is largely shaped by the administrative milieux in which (these 'intermediary strata') are located" (Petras, 1976b:433). In essence, it is state-capitalism.

One of state-capitalism's central features is national control—nationalization—of profitable enterprises. Thus, the Arab military-bureaucratic "intermediary strata" in Egypt and Syria quickly initiated political economic policies—such as nationalization of Western interests and arms purchases from the East European bloc—which clashed with the U.S.-Israel interests in the region. Indeed, these strata gained popularity and support from among the masses in direct relation to the degree of their resistance to Zionism and imperialism and to the degree they promised to liberate Palestine. And their popularity was enormous, since spectacular politico-military events confirmed the determination of the new rulers to fight against foreign domination.

Most prominently in Egypt, then in Syria and Iraq, the emergent anti-Zionist and anti-imperialist struggle of these strata quickly pitted them against the remaining local Arab allies of imperialism—the ruling classes of the oil-producing regions of the Arab east. Thus, an Arab cold war, reflecting in part the international cold war, ensued in the 1950s which soon turned into a hot confrontation in a remote and seemingly unimportant corner of the Arab world: Yemen (see Kerr, 1971). The war in Yemen in the early 1960s was between Egypt and Saudi Arabia, client states of the Soviet Union and the United States respectively, fought both by proxy and directly.[1]

The Arab periphery came to be seen by Marxist and bourgeois analysts alike as being divided into two main antagonistic camps: pro-imperialist (oil producing) states in the Arabian peninsula and North Africa in alliance with the Hashemite monarchy of Jordan against anti-imperialist, "Arab socialist" regimes in Egypt, Syria, and Iraq (joined later by Algeria, Libya, and even the Sudan). Wrought with contradictions these two camps joined forces and became bitterly divided in a series of politico-military confrontations with Israel and Britain, France and the United States.

During that period (1950s to the mid-1960s) the foreign policy of the state-capitalist regimes of Egypt and Syria became strongly anti-imperialist (including joining the nonaligned and other third world blocs). Their domestic policy strengthened the "public sector" (a euphemism for state-capitalist investment) and restricted the private sector, especially to the penetration of foreign capital. Likewise, their international economic policies defined the terms of trade and economic relations with the West. During this period they tilted increasingly toward the East European bloc.

Domestically they initiated investment in capital goods industry in order to lay the foundation for a national economy, all according to the theory of "noncapitalist development," as their Soviet and Soviet trained advisers called it. This is a theoretically necessary stage in order to create the foundation for the *socialist* road.[2]

Increasingly dependent upon and allied with the Soviet Union these state-capitalist regimes captured the imagination of the Arab masses as they opposed and frequently defeated imperialist and Zionist pressures—overt, covert, economic, diplomatic, political, and even military. For example, the 1956 Suez War military defeat was turned into a diplomatic and political victory by Nasser's regime. Thus the hopes of the Arab masses for national liberation including economic betterment became anchored on these state-capitalist regimes,[3] especially Nasser's Egypt.

POLITICAL-ECONOMIC REVERSALS
OF STATE CAPITALISM

In June 1967, in six days of war with Israel, these state-capitalist regimes collapsed militarily. Since then, these regimes whose policies had been anti-imperialist and anti-private capital, and whose rhetoric was revolutionary, began to exhibit a series of political-economic reversals domestically, regionally, and internationally.

Political concessions to both imperialism and Zionism accelerated enormously after the October 1973 War under Sadat of Egypt and Assad of Syria. Indeed, these regimes pursued policies and took postures which have been in contradiction with the resurgent and now independent Palestine national liberation movement. These regimes came in conflict with the very movement of the people whose homeland they long promised to liberate. In short, these political reversals and concessions slowly and then dramatically turned into counterrevolutionary policies.

Here it is both necessary and instructive to document the political-economic reversals and counterrevolutionary activities of the principal state-capitalist regimes: Egypt and Syria. However, in order to understand that fully, a comment on the post-1967 Arab/Palestinian revolutionary thrust is in order. With the 1967 military collapse of the state-capitalist regimes two simultaneous political tendencies emerged in the Arab east. One, spearheaded by the Palestinian movement, proposed and practiced mass armed revolutionary mobilization with socialist ideology as the only path to true national pan-Arab independence and the liberation of Palestine; the other, led by Saudi Arabia, called for liquidation of Arab communism (Arab revolution), strong alliance with and integration into American imperialism, and the use of diplomatic/political/financial pressure as the means to restore Arab lands from Israeli occupation. Its most potent weapon has been financial, providing credits and funds for the fiscally and economically crisis-ridden state-capitalisms of Egypt and Syria. Despite the defiant tone of the 1967 Khartoum Arab summit conference, the content of the declarations heralded precisely the beginning of the political-economic reversals. In the first place, national liberation and the liberation of Palestine were *redefined* as the regaining of Arab territory lost in the June 1967 war with Israel. Implicitly it meant the abandonment of the principal Arab/Palestinian goal of the total liberation of Palestine, and the acceptance of Israel as a settler-colonial state in the region.

In 1969 Nasser accepted Secretary of State William Rogers's plan for political settlement of the Middle East conflict, a plan which would guarantee the security and recognition of Israel and the denial of Palestinian national rights. In 1970 the Jordan army of King Hussein attacked the Palestinian guerrillas in a savage war in Amman and the rest of Jordan. The Egyptian and Iraqi state-capitalist regimes had troops in Jordan but did not intervene on the side of the Palestinians. Only Syria entered halfheartedly to help the Palestinians—a tank brigade moved into Jordan but received no air cover. The commander of the Syrian air force refused to support the intervention. That commander was Hafez al-Assad, the current president of Syria. In turn, this half-hearted intervention precipitated an internal Syrian struggle within factions of the ruling Baath party. The *right wing*, the wing of the anti-Marxist Hafez Al-Assad, won. By 1971 a similar struggle ensued in Egypt, leading also to the hegemony of the right wing faction of the state-capitalist ruling strata. There, Anwar Al-Sadat won over Ali Sabri, a pro-Soviet, more anti-Western state capitalist. In Egypt this struggle culminated in expulsion of over 20,000 Soviet advisors and opened the door to the American connection. Also, in the early 1970s an Anglo-Iranian and Saudi Arab-Jordan intervention in Dhofar/Oman liquidated the victories of the revolutionary forces in southern Arabia. In 1974, the state-regime of Jaafar Nimeri in Sudan brutally put down, with the help of Egype and Libya, an attempted coup by military elements, some of whom were members of the Sudanese Communist Party. What followed was a massacre of Sudanese communists on a smaller scale but not unlike the pattern of Suharto's Indonesia. However, the most dramatic example of these reversals is the Syrian regime's intervention in Lebanon on the side of the Lebanese *rightists* and against the alliance of the Lebanese *leftists* and the Palestinians. Seen as the principal revolutionary cadres and revolutionary catalyst in the region, the Palestinians suffered heavy losses and were contained militarily and politically by the army of a state—Syria—long the Palestinians' staunchest ally and most inveterate anti-imperialist and anti-Zionist country in the Arab world. This Syrian war against the Palestinian and Lebanese revolutionary cadres was waged with the apparent blessing of the United States and the tacit acceptance of Egypt and Saudi Arabia. This counterrevolutionary effort was in alliance, on the one hand, with local counterrevolutionary parties and militias in Lebanon and, on the other, internationally with direct and indirect coordination with the U.S. and Israel respectively.[4]

The content of this Arab counterrevolution in the state-capitalist regimes is not merely political but is also economic and social in character. In both Egypt and Syria repression of worker-peasant activism and other dissent has been quick and severe. State-capitalist policies, laws, and institutions were abandoned and dismantled. For example, some state-owned enterprises were resold to private capital as private investment, including foreign—especially American—capital was encouraged (Aulas, 1976).

In short, restoration of private capital, integration into and political collaboration with American imperialism coupled with regional counterrevolution has become the policy of these state-capitalist regimes. These are policies not unlike those of the oil-producing states of the Arabian peninsula. Originally anti-imperialist, Egyptian and Syrian state-capitalism turned pro-imperialist; originally anti-Zionist, they turned anti-Palestinian;[5] originally progressive and seemingly "revolutionary," they turned distinctly repressive and counterrevolutionary.

STATE CAPITALISM IN CRISIS: A THESIS

The problem of this paper, then, is: What are the conditions that brought about such sociopolitical reversals? That is, what are the conditions responsible for counterrevolution in the contemporary Arab periphery?

The answer to this question, needless to say, is complex and involves analysis of the dynamics of the political economy of the world system as it triggers both regional and local dynamics in a particular part of the world capitalist periphery. In the 20th century, counterrevolution is global in scope and is practiced overtly and covertly by the leading imperialist power, the United States (See Klare, 1972; Petras and Morley, 1976; Halliday, 1975; MERIP Reports, 1972, 1975). Counter-revolution also emerges locally, as in the right wing movements in Lebanon (see Farsoun and Carroll, 1976).

Our task here is to analyze the conditions which generate counterrevolution in state-capitalist regimes in the Arab world. The thesis of this paper is that the national and regional triumph of counterrevolution in the Arab periphery is derived from the *crisis*, perhaps dissolution, of state-capitalism as a mode of accumulation and growth in Egypt and Syria (see Mendes, 1975). Iraq, Libya, and Algeria, also state-capitalist regimes, remain anti-capitalist only because their extensive and profitable oil resources continue to be a "successful" mode of accumulation. Even they, in the face of rising regional counterrevolution, have significantly modified their radical nationalist militancy. The internal contradictions of state-capitalism in Egypt and Syria determined both the limits of their respective socioeconomic development and the trans-formation of their political posture from anti-imperialism to counterrevolution. Thus, the reversals are the objective expression of the vested interests of the "intermediary strata" of state-capitalism during the period of crisis. The principal contradictions of Egyptian and Syrian state-capitalism are indeed the same as those listed by Petras in general for state-capitalist society: "conflict between dependence on advanced technology/marginalization of labor, between industrial expansion/modernization, between bureaucratic appropriation/exploitation of productive sectors" (Petras, 1976a:30).

EGYPTIAN STATE CAPITALISM: AN EXAMPLE[6]

The coup d'état of the Free Officers movement led by Nasser in 1952 resolved the crisis of neo-colonial capitalist development in the face of rising popular and mass based activism during that period. For, in 1952, the National Planning Committee in Egypt declared its role to "prepare the proper conditions for the growth and encouragement of private capital and the blossoming of free individual projects" (Mendes, 1975:103). The Egyptian Free Officers declared their intentions to

(1) provide encouragement for private investment into industrial interprises;

(2) grant corporate tax exemptions for seven years, and also tax exemptions for profit from new stocks in established companies for five years (currently, undistributed dividends are also tax exempt for 50% of their value);

(3) expand tariff protection for industry;

(4) encourage savings among small capitalists and reduce the minimum value of a stock from 4 to 2.

By 1954, the chairman of the board of the Ah-Ahli bank stated that "the feelings of anxiety and fear among businessmen have disappeared during 1954" (Mendes, 1975:103-104).

State investment in the industrial sector in Egypt only began in the mid-1950s as a result of the failure of private Egyptian capital to invest there. Private capital continued to invest in traditional sectors reaping rapid profit as a consequence. For example, investment in real estate rose from E£40 million in 1954 to E£51.4 million in 1959. Most important, a decrease in the value of fixed-capital formation took place in the private sector from E£113 million in 1949 to E£76 million in 1959 (Hussein, 1969). Thus, the failure of private capital to build the industrial capitalist base and the entry of state-capital into the industrial and other sectors led to a rise in the importance and role of state-capitalists. It also set in motion contradictions with private capital in this mode of accumulation which came to be resolved in favor of state-capital because of direct link to executive power. The Nasserist *National Charter*, with its "socialist" measures, is the legal document which signified the victory of state-capitalism. And through Soviet aid and advice, Egyptian "intermediary strata" began transforming the forces of production and building a more efficient mode of accumulation. It is during this period of its rise that Egyptian state-capitalism became anti-imperialist and supported nationalist-revolutionary and democratic movements in the Arab world.

But Egyptian state capitalism quickly exhibited internal contradictions similar to those listed by Petras. A parasitic overexpansion of the bureaucratic-administrative sector ensued, especially in high positions. There was an increase of 61% in the number of bureaucrats and a 215% increase in their incomes between 1962-1966. Meanwhile, blue-collar occupations decreased in the same period.

In 1962-1966, there was an increase in consumption in the state sector of 55.2% in contrast to an increase of only 17.2% in the private (individual) sector (Egyptian Communist, n.d.:10). Another author provides the following data: the salaries of those in high positions increased by 230% while their numbers increased by 415%, and the gap between the highest and lowest wage in the administrative hierarchy increased 40 times. This new prosperity among the state-capitalists led to a rapid demand for consumer goods albeit restricted largely to these strata. In turn, this caused increasing investment in consumer goods industry and allied import substitution industries. Analysis of individual consumption indicates an increase in assembled luxury goods (electrical and other appliances) rather than food and other necessities.

Additionally, in the first five year plan of the early 1960s, the planned increase in the services sector was overfulfilled by 135%, while in agriculture only 63.1% of the planned increase was achieved. And 49.5% of the planned increase was achieved in industry (Egyptian Communist, n.d.:10).

In general, one can say that Egyptian state-capitalism failed to follow through with its project of developing the national forces of production as the new ruling strata asserted their economic and consumer interests. This was restricted in scope to these new strata and hardly reached the increasingly impoverished masses. A crisis of state capitalism begins to set in by the mid-sixties. A crisis of marketing increased inventories enormously, for example on June 30, 1966, the value of inventories was E£78 million, while on June 30, 1967, it was E£100 and on June 30, 1968 it was E£121 million. Additionally, unused capacity reached E£121.5 in the state industrial sector in 1968-1969 and E£200 in 1973. Furthermore, the deficit in balance of payments in 1964-1965 rose to E£135 million and totaled E£417 million at the end of the first five year plan that ended in 1965. Finally, the official rate of unemployment, let alone underemployment and hidden unemployment, increased from 7.6% in 1964-1965 to 8.5% in 1967-1977 at the time of the June War (Egyptian Communist, n.d.:10-11).

Thus, the crisis of Egyptian state-capitalism became especially acute as Egypt was defeated militarily in six days in 1967, and all of Sinai came under Israeli occupation. The way out of this crisis seemed to be in "concessions" to U.S. imperialism and its regional allies (Saudi Arabia and other Gulf states), who could extend funds to pull the ruling state-capitalist strata from their fiscal dilemmas. This process was not restricted to Egypt but included Syria as well.

In short, state-capitalist ruling strata in Egypt and Syria are unable to resolve their fundamentally capitalist crisis especially sharpened by the Arab-Israeli wars, nor to resolve their contradiction with the exploited and restive peasants and workers. To survive, they open the door to Western imperialism, local reaction, and initiate counterrevolution.

STATE CAPITALISM AND THE NEW CLASSES

The rise of the "intermediary strata" leads to elimination of the landlord class and the big bourgeoisie. But their transformation of the productive forces through state capital evolves according to the laws of motion of capitalist institutions and the capitalist market both domestically and in the world system. Even the land reform leads to the development in the rural areas of a *Kulak* class which continues to exploit the peasantry, perhaps more efficiently than the old semi-feudal landlords. Around the state sector a *new* bourgeois class—contractors, consultants, import and export specialists, distributors, as well as the expanded military-bureaucratic establishment—develops. These new bourgeois and parasitic classes are literally the *creation* of state-capitalism. Their interests and their consciousness are fundamentally capitalist and contrary to the further development of socialism. As they become economically and politically influential, they disrupt the socialists' path. As they accumulate capital surplus they put pressure on the state-capitalist strata for opening the door to private, including foreign, capital. Their voices and ideology become relevant for state-capitalists especially as the fiscal crises deepen and as the workers-peasants exhibit restiveness and become a threat. In alliance with the right-wing factions of the ruling intermediary state-capitalist strata they impel revisions in policy leading to a bloodless coup against the left-wing faction (i.e., Ali Sabri and Salah Jadid in Egypt and Syria, respectively).

This new class alliance has two important political consequences: domestically it restricts democratic freedoms and worker movements, and internationally it opens the door to Western imperialism, drawing away economically and politically from the strong links to the Eastern and Soviet bloc. The sum of these two developments translates into counterrevolution in the country and in the region.

What helps this process of "regression" is the cultural and ideological legacies of colonialism and neocolonialism. It is both individualistic and opportunistic. Even the state apparatus suffers from these potentialities, and corruption quickly sets in. Egyptian and Syrian state-capitalist ruling strata are notorious for their corruption (Aulas, 1976; Randall, 1977). In short, "state-capitalism, while exhibiting many of the common external features of socialist development, is in reality the imposition of new forms on old structures, leading to a socio-economic impasse in which the old 'structures' increasingly inform the newer forms" (Petras, 1976a:22).

CONCLUSION

In the Arab periphery state-capitalism emerged as a mode of production of the "intermediary strata" which was the means for resolving the crisis of dependent capitalism. Precisely because of the neocolonial linkage of dependent capitalists, the resolution of the crisis through state capitalism turns these states to anti-imperialism in the initial period of establishment and ascendency of the leading "intermediary strata." It is especially so in the Arab world, going beyond economic nationalism, because of Israel and the prominence of the national question. Ascendent state-capitalism and its leading strata rally the masses, divert them from a revolutionary path, and mediate between them and the discredited bourgeoisie. However, the state-capitalist project triggers its own internal contradictions and is unable to resolve either the national or class questions. (Again, in the Arab periphery, the threat of Israel sharpens the failure and crisis of Egyptian and Syrian state-capitalism.) The state-capitalist ruling strata, in alliance with a new parasitical bourgeoisie and the resurgent old bourgeoisie fears displacement or destruction at the hands of mass-based revolutionary movements. They thus seek salvation via counter-revolution and integration into imperialism.

In a sense, in the period of stagnation or crisis and decline, state-capitalism becomes at the very least repressive of proletarian-peasant movements but becomes fully counterrevolutionary when the threat is genuine. Counterrevolution domestically and regionally is but a symptom of the political-economic reversals. Indeed, these reversals lead to the destruction of state-capitalism as a mode of accumulation and the emergence of a more rapacious and more repressive dependent capitalist mode (as is the process in Egypt and Syria currently in the Arab periphery). So long as this new mode contains the revolutionary thrust it will receive the multi-lateral and multi-varied aid of imperialism and reaction. (Recall the U.S. government's action at the time of the recent Cairo food riots and continuing aid to Sadat's regime). However, the future of state capitalism is tenuous. For its demise will come either at the hands of another group of "intermediate strata," which sets the anti-imperialist/pro-imperialist cycle in motion again, or at the hands of a revolutionary party representing the interests of the proletariat and peasantry.

In Egypt, at least, indications of this latter development already emerged in the food riots of January 1977 and in the reestablishment of the Egyptian Communist Party and other left of center movements. In the Arab periphery, the leadership of the national liberation struggle may now be falling into the hands of the revolutionary proletarian movements as both the bourgeoisie, the petite bourgeoisie and "intermediary strata" have discredited themselves.

The fusion of the national and class questions in such a clear manner augurs an Arab "civil war"[7] and potential proletarian national liberation movement which will in the future liberate Palestine from Zionism and the Arab world from imperialism. Otherwise, a rightist regional hegemony anchored on an axis of Arab oil states, the U.S., and Israel will form, as state-capitalist regimes transform and integrate themselves into this new counterrevolutionary situation. This conjuncture would entail its own contradictions which could render its stability problematic.

NOTES

1. The consequences of the Yemen conflict are rather interesting as two Yemeni states emerged, one neocolonial (Yemen Arab Republic) and the other socialist (People's Democratic Republic of Yemen); see Stork (1973) and Al-Ashtal (1975). See also Halliday (1975).

2. These regimes called themselves "Arab Socialist," "Algerian Socialist," or simply "Arab Nationalist" on the road to building socialism.

3. The activity of the communist parties concentrated heavily on trade union organizing and on bread and butter issues and ignored the national liberation question, especially the liberation of Palestine. Thus, they hardly attracted the masses or appealed to them.

4. Sheehan (1976), a Kissinger admirer, sees this active collaboration between Syria, Israel, and the U.S. versus the Palestinians as a coincidence at a certain juncture of strategic interests.

5. Accomodationist to Israel and containing the Palestinian movement.

6. We are currently gathering more data on Egypt and, especially, on Syria.

7. The form that this Arab "civil war" will take will be varied, ranging from the classic variety of Lebanon to the Egyptian-Libyan military confrontation of summer 1977.

REFERENCES

AL-ASHTAL, A. (1976). "Politics in command: A case study of the People's Democratic Republic of Yemen." Monthly Review, 27(February):13-21.

AULAS, M.-C. (1976). "Sadat's Egypt." New Left Review, 98:84-95.

Egyptian Communist (pseudonym, n.d.). Tabi'at al-Sultah wa qadiyat al-Tahaluf al-Tabaqi fi Misr (Nature of Power and the question of Class Alliance in Egypt). Beirut: Dar Al-Taliah.

FARSOUN, S.K., and CARROLL, W.F. (1976). "The civil war in Lebanon: Sect, class, and imperialism." Monthly Review, 28(June):12-37.

HALLIDAY, F. (1975). Arabia without sultans: A survey of political instability in the Arab world. New York: Random House Vintage.

HUSSEIN, M.A-F. (1969). Dirasat Arabiyya (September).

KERR, M. (1971). The Arab cold war. London: Oxford University Press.

KLARE, M. (1972). War without end: American planning for the next Vietnams. New York: Random House Vintage.

LEYS, C. (1977). "Notes on development theory." Journal of Contemporary Asia, 7.

MAYER, A.J. (1971). Dynamics of counterrevolution in Europe, 1870-1956. New York: Harper.

MENDES, H. (1975). "Hawl Tabi'at al-Sultah fi Misr" (About the Nature of Power in Egypt). Al-Mawaqif, 63(December):17-18.

MERIP Reports (1972). "The U.S. in Jordan: The thrice rescued throne." No. 7, February.

MERIP Reports (1975). "America's Shah, Shahanshah's Iran." No. 36, April.

MERIP Reports (1975). "Neo-piracy in Oman and the Gulf." No. 40, September.

PETRAS, J.F. (1976a). "Class and politics in the periphery and the transition to socialism." Review of Radical Political Economics, 8(2):20-35.

——— (1976b). "State capitalism and the third world." Journal of Contemporary Asia, 6:432-443.

PETRAS, J.F., and MORLEY, M. (1976). The United States and Chile. New York: Monthly Review.

RANDALL, J. (1977). "Assad acts to restore image shaken by corruption, unrest." Washington Post, September 23.

SHEEHAN, E.R.F. (1976). "From unity to discord in Araby." Washington Post, August 15, C1-C2.

STORK, J. (1973). "Socialist revolution in Arabia: A report from the People's Democratic Republic of Yemen." MERIP Reports, 15:1-25.

TILLY, C. (1964). The Vendée. Cambridge: Harvard University Press.

WELTY, G., and BOWMAN, S. (forthcoming). "Capitalisme, colonialisme, et corporatisme," L'homme et la société. Paris.

PART 3

THE WORLD SYSTEM IN THE 20TH CENTURY

Chapter 6

CORE-PERIPHERY RELATIONS:
THE EFFECTS OF CORE COMPETITION

Christopher Chase-Dunn

Recent work on the theory of capitalist development tries to extend Marx's accumulation model to include the state system, the world market, and class struggle at the world level (Wallerstein, 1974; Amin, 1976; Mandel, 1975). Wallerstein has emphasized the importance of studying the whole system in which capitalism operates, the world-economy, composed of interacting classes, firms, nation-states, and a geographical division of labor between core states and peripheral areas.

This paper is a theoretical discussion of the effects of economic competition and development among core states in the world-system on the structure of core-periphery relations.[1]

Capitalist development takes place unevenly, not only creating the gap between core and periphery, but also tending to concentrate productive advantage in a particular core state. As Wallerstein (1974: 350) says, "it may well be that in this

Author's Note: I would like to thank Richard Rubinson and Albert J. Bergesen for their help on this paper.

kind of system it is not structurally possible to avoid, over a long period of time, a circulation of the elites in the sense that the particular country that is dominant at a given time tends to be replaced in this role sooner or later by another country." Competitive advantage in production and exchange have concentrated in three core states since the birth of the capitalist world-system in the 16th century—the United Provinces (Netherlands) in the 17th century, the United Kingdom in the 19th century, and the United States in the 20th century. During the period of their economic hegemony each of these core states attained a high level of productivity and capital accumulation relative to other areas. Such periods of concentration are followed by a dispersion of the economic conditions which made the hegemony possible to other competing core states.

It should be emphasized that hegemony in the core of the capitalist world-system is not a matter of relative military power. First Spain and then France were more powerful than other single states in terms of state revenues or the ability to mount military expeditions. Hegemony is rather a matter of the combination of coercive power and economic competitive advantage. It is the ability to produce goods or render services cheaply, in combination with a degree of military power which enables the capitalists of a hegemonic core state to realize greater profits in the world market. This is neither the peaceful realm of free market competition painted by liberal economics, nor is it the direct extraction of surplus product through coercion which characterized the precapitalist empires.

From a structural perspective the distribution of competitive advantage in production between core states can be viewed as alternating between two forms: (1) a unicentric form in which there is a clearly hegemonic core state, and (2) a multicentric form in which competitive advantage in production is more evenly spread across the states of the core. These can be diagrammed as follows:

0
0000   00000
Unicentric   Multicentric

The claim here is that over time the structure of competitive advantage in the core alternates from relative unicentricity to relative multicentricity as hegemonic core states rise and fall.

The causes of the rise and fall of hegemonic core states are not the main focus of this paper, but a discussion of them may be helpful. In general, this "circulation" can be understood as a result of the unevenness of capital accumulation in the context of the state system (competing "sovereign" and unequally powerful territorial nation-states) which comprises the political organizations of the capitalist world-system. First let us focus on the causes of the rise of a particular core state. Concentration of productive advantage is partly due to locational advantages which interact favorably with the level of technology and organization appropriate to the scale of the world economy during a particular era. Centrality in the world economy is facilitated by geographical centrality, especially when transport costs are high. Reflecting on the hegemony of the United Provinces, the United Kingdom, and the United States suggests that there is a rough correspondence between the size of the home market and the scale of the world-economy. Balance between the size of internal and external markets appears important. Countries may be both too little and too large to contend for the position of hegemonic core state.

The political conditions which enable a state to specialize in core activities have been discussed by Rubinson (Chapter 2 in this volume). To become hegemonic requires a strong coalition of national class interests vis-à-vis the world economy and a strong state willing to pursue international economic and political objectives. Military advantage is important, but it is usually combined with alliances with other states against contending powers. The British defeat of Napoleon and the Dutch balancing of the great powers against one another serve as examples. It is striking that hegemony in the core is consolidated after wars in which potential contenders have destroyed one another.

Now let us look at the causes of the evening out of productive advantage across the core. Successful accumulation creates investment capital which searches for profitable opportunities in other core states, facilitating their development. British railroad building, Dutch participation in the English East India Company, and U.S. corporations in Europe serve as examples. Successful accumulation also leads to political demands, the expansion of "unproductive" activities, and the development of labor organization which can effectively obtain higher wages. These demands and constraints on capital are articulated primarily through the apparatus of the territorial nation-state, and because there is no larger world state overarching the world economy, capital can always escape to areas where opposition is less.[2] Foreign investment in the context of a competitive state system is a risky business, however. It may bring higher profits in the short run, but it is also subject to expropriation in areas outside the jurisdiction of the investing country. This is, in part, why hegemonic core states have not been able to maintain their positions indefinitely through the means of foreign investment.

The turnover time of fixed capital is another factor which causes the decline of hegemonic core states. Heavy investment (at a particular level of technological productivity) in fixed capital, such as plant shells, transportation systems, urban infrastructure, and so forth commits a national economy to utilize that fixed capital over a period of time, during which competing producers in other nations can acquire more productive and competitive fixed capital.

Another factor in the decline of hegemonic states is the "international" costs which accompany hegemony. The world economy requires some investment in the maintenance of monetary and coercive institutions, and these costs tend to fall disproportionately on the hegemonic core power, especially during the later stages of the hegemony (Szymanski, 1973).

Hegemony based on productive advantage enables a core state to become central in world commerce and finance. This centrality is retained long after the advantage in production has diffused to competing core states (Wallerstein, forthcoming).

Thus Amsterdam, London, and New York remain financial world centers long after the decline of their national competitive advantage in production.

Let us now turn to the effects of changes in the distribution of economic power among core states on the structure of control and exchange between the core and the periphery of the world-system. The relationship between the core and the periphery involves a division of labor which is maintained, in part, by a structure of power-dependence relations. The transfer of surplus product from the periphery to the core, the class alliances, infrastructure, and political regimes created by this division of labor act to reproduce it (Chase-Dunn and Rubinson, 1976). But the core-periphery control structure alternates between a more or less multilateral system of "free" trade on the one hand, and a more bilateral, particularistic system of colonial empires on the other. These two structures are illustrated by Figure 1.

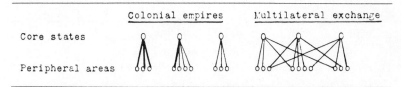

Figure 1. CORE-PERIPHERY CONTROL STRUCTURE

This figure illustrates two structures of control and exchange between core states and peripheral areas. In the system of colonial empires each core state monopolizes the exchange with its own colonies and excludes other core states from this trade. In the multilateral structure, trade is less controlled by mercantilist state policies and the exchange comes closer to the ideal of a world market. These schematic alternatives are complicated in reality by the fact that new areas are brought into the periphery of the world-system as it expands. The economic penetration by chartered companies, individual entrepreneurs, colonial settlers, and the formal establishment of colonies by the core states expanded to include the whole globe by the end of the 19th century. This expansion of core-periphery relations must be included in the model along with changes in the structure of core-periphery trade. Also, we must consider the development of resistance to core exploitation in the periphery. It is necessary to distinguish between resistance from *external* arenas and resistance from peripheral areas *within* the world-economy. External arenas, or areas not yet brought into the effective division of labor which is the world-economy (Wallerstein, 1974), often are capable of preventing penetration (e.g., the Moghul Empire in India before the 19th century). Resistance which emerges from peripheral areas within the world-economy (e.g., decolonization movements, restrictions on the penetration of investment capital, the growth of labor organizations, international trade cartels, etc.) is a response to the process of capitalist development and reflects back on that process. This is a manifestation of class struggle at the level of the world-economy as a whole.

In addition to the uneven development of core powers it is important to consider the effects of the rate of aggregate economic growth in the world economy as a whole, and also the level of political and military conflict between core powers. Our structural model will include these variables as well as those discussed above: changes in the structure of core-periphery trade, expansion and deepening of economic exploitation of the periphery, expansion of colonial empires, and the development of resistance to the core. We will try to specify the causal relationships between these structural characteristics of the world-system, but first let us discuss a broader theoretical perspective.

THE MODE OF PRODUCTION IN THE WORLD-SYSTEM

Wallerstein has argued that the mode of production is a feature of the world-system as a whole, rather than of only part of the interactive whole. This is a break with Marx's conception of the fully developed capitalist mode of production, which by definition applies only to production in which labor is juridically "free" and divorced from ownership or control of the means of production. Marx focused on the core of the system, and based his model of capital accumulation on the assumption that the institutions and state structures which were characteristic of this segment would eventually spread across national boundaries to the rest of the world. As he said in the Preface to Volume 1 of *Capital*, "the country that is more developed industrially only shows, to the less developed, the image of its own future." He saw colonialism as a passing phase which enabled European capitalism to get its start—the plunder of "primitive accumulation"—or which helped to spread the capitalist mode of production to new areas. He did not perceive the extent to which the core-periphery dimension and primitive accumulation are a permanent and functional part of the system as a whole.

Wallerstein, following the dependency theorists, has reconceptualized the theory of capitalist development in terms of the systematic way in which state structures are related to production relations. He argues that the capitalist mode of production includes not only free labor, but also coerced labor (capitalist slavery, serfdom, or other forms of labor control) in which the state plays a more direct part. Of course Marx was the first to point out that the juridical freedom of proletarians is an institutionalized mystification hiding the extraction of surplus value. The role of the state in the exploitation of slaves or serfs engaged in the production of commodities for sale on the world market is only a more apparent example of the immersion of part of the state structure in production relations (Poulantzas, 1975; Mandel, 1975). Thus, Wallerstein defines the capitalist mode of production as production for profit in the world market in which labor is a commodity, but is not necessarily paid a "wage." The surplus value which is extracted from peasants (or slaves) engaged in commodity production, or that which is transferred from the periphery to the core by the mechanism of "unequal exchange" analyzed by Emmanuel (1972), continues to play an important part in the accumulation of capital. Uneven development and the core-periphery division of labor are normal consequences of the accumulation process. They also perform important functions in reproducing the conditions for accumulation by reinforcing the state system. This allows capital to be mobile by dividing the loyalties of exploited classes across the system.

COMPETITION AND POLITICAL CONTROL

The political structure of this mode of production is a system of formally sovereign nation-states which are organizations within a larger economic network. It is very important to the maneuverability of capital that there be no single state structure which encompasses the entire world economy. Attempts to impose a single unified state on the whole system have repeatedly failed, and capitalism continues to develop precisely because capital can escape the political control of classes that emerge in opposition to it. States are organizations by which classes interfere with markets, or leave them to operate competitively, depending on the advantages to the class or classes controlling the state. A class which has a purely economic competitive advantage in the world market will advocate free trade among core powers and use its power to enforce the "open door" in peripheral areas (Robinson and Gallagher, 1953). The ideology of economic liberalism was clearly articulated by Grotius and de Witt during the Dutch hegemony of the 17th century (Wilson, 1957). Also, classes dependent on the export of raw materials to the core in exchange for manufactured goods will advocate and enforce free trade. Classes at a competitive disadvantage try to protect their share of the surplus by using state power to influence market exchange and production.

This understanding of the interaction between political control and market advantage derives from Polanyi's (1944) analysis of capitalist development as a process in which production escapes political control and then is recaptured by the emergence of political opposition to the "market mentality." The "caretaker" state of 19th century Britain is the regime of a class in power than controls a purely economic competitive advantage in the world market. As its advantage slips away, it employs the state more and more frequently to protect its declining share of the surplus. In the world-system as a whole, periods of general economic expansion are those in which exchange is relatively "free," whereas periods of contraction or stagnation are characterized by a much more "mercantilist" or state-protected system of exchange. Cycles of this kind can be seen throughout the history of capitalist development.

Thus the institutional separation between the economic and political, which is fundamental to capitalism, is largely a feature of the world-economy as a whole. At this level the arena of competition, the world market, is divided up by a multiplicity of competing and conflicting states, the so-called "international system." State power is often used to facilitate the appropriation of surplus value, but this in no way alters the disjuncture between the political and the economic. In this light the rise of "state monopoly capitalism" in the 20th century is not really a fundamental change in the structure of the system. The expansion of the economic functions of the state within the national economy does not change the competitive functioning of the world market. Only the establishment of a state which overarches the whole system can reintegrate the economic and the political.

Within this theoretical perspective, then, we seek to investigate some of the functions of primitive accumulation for the development of capitalism. For Marx, primitive accumulation was the method by which the institutions of capitalism were created. The creation of a proletariat, the creation of capitalist agriculture, the accumulation of bullion by the plunder or precapitalist areas, and the creation of a world market by "merchant capital" were all necessary precursors to expanded reproduction which involved the use of coercive state power in one or another form (Marx, 1967). Amin (1976) makes the point that primitive accumulation also plays an important role in allowing "normal" wage labor exploitation to proceed in core countries.[3] Thus the conditions for primitive accumulation are not transitory but are reproduced, especially in the periphery, resulting in the "development of underdevelopment" or the reproduction of seemingly "precapitalist" forms (Amin, 1976).

It may be said without contradiction that both Marx and Amin are right. Primitive accumulation in the sense of the use of coercive state power for the appropriation of surplus does continue to play an important role, but also its more blatant forms (e.g., capitalist slavery, serfdom, and formal colonialism) have been replaced with forms more closely akin to "free labor" (e.g., unequal exchange, support of repressive peripheral regimes, and other forms of neocolonialism). Thus, while production relations still remain differentiated across the core-periphery dimension, they are becoming relatively more homogeneous over the long run. The importance of this is suggested by Wallerstein's contention that "when labor is everywhere free we shall have socialism" (1974:127).

Now let us focus on a particular aspect of primitive accumulation, the structure of coercion between the core and the periphery, to try to understand how alterations in this structure are caused by and affect the process of accumulation in the core. Intensive and extensive development are always alternatives for capital and their relative profitability is determined in part by the level of resistance which is encountered. Thus one reason that capital is exported to the periphery and that colonial expansion is undertaken is that resistance is less there. Also expanded reproduction in the core creates demand for products which can be cheaply produced in the periphery.

And core producers seek market outlets in colonial areas. All these stimulate the use of core political power against resistance in the periphery. In addition, and more directly related to the topic of this research, competition between core powers encourages defensive expansion of colonial empires.

CORE COMPETITION AND THE
STRUCTURE OF CORE-PERIPHERY RELATIONS

The specific world-system level process we seek to investigate is the way in which competition among core states and their national bourgeoisies affects the relationship between the core and the periphery. The descriptive form of the hypothesis is that a "unicentric" distribution of productive advantage in the core, in which the bourgeoisie of a single core state dominates the accumulation process, leads to a relatively multilateral structure of exchange and control between the core and the periphery and the relaxation of political controls over core-periphery exchange. Another way of stating this is to say that a "multicentric" distribution of competitive advantage in the core leads to a bilateral structure of exchange and control between core states and their colonial empires and also to the expansion of colonial empires to new territories. This relationship is schematically illustrated in Figure 2. The aggregate rate of economic growth in the world-economy as a whole is another variable which is systematically related to uneven development among core states and the structure of core-periphery relations. This is not conceptually independent of the relative rates of growth in core powers, but neither is it completely reduceable to these rates. Economic production has grown in a cyclical (or periodic) fashion since the emergence of the capitalist system, and the rate of this growth, whether speeding up or slowing down, affects the level of conflict among core powers and the tendency to use political coercion in accumulation. During periods of economic expansion

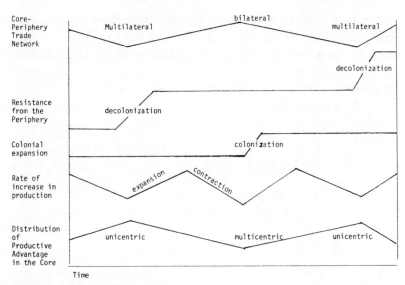

Figure 2. DESCRIPTIVE MODEL

the aggregate amount of surplus value is increasing and relatively peaceful economic competition is the main method by which this surplus is appropriated. On the other hand, in periods of contraction, classes with access to state power will actively employ it to protect their shares of a shrinking pie. This contextual variable (the rate of increase in aggregate world economic growth, which is illustrated in Figure 2 net of the secular absolute increase) interacts with changes in the distribution of competitive advantage in the core to produce shifts in the structure of core-periphery relations.

Let us decompose the process of uneven development in the core into three parts: (1) the growth of production in the hegemonic core state resulting from the concentration of productive advantages; (2) the growth of production in competing core states resulting from the evening out of the distribution of productive advantage; and (3) the aggregate rate of economic development in the world-economy.

Similarly, we can decompose the core-periphery relationship into four components: (1) economic penetration of peripheral areas by core entrepreneurs; (2) expansion of formal colonial control; (3) the alternation between a bilateral and multilateral network of exchange between the core and periphery; and (4) the growth of peripheral resistance as manifested by decolonization movements and other constraints on core domination.

The relationship between these two sets of variables is mediated in part by the level of conflict between core states. These variables and the hypothesized causal relations between them are illustrated in Figure 3.

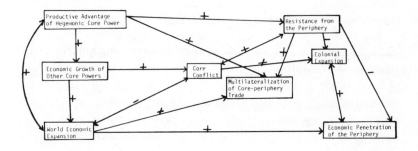

Figure 3. CAUSAL MODEL

The concentration of productive advantage in a single core state means that commodities are being produced at a low cost and in enough volume to invade old markets and create new ones. When the price of these commodities is low enough, and demand in other core countries is high enough, the political interests restricting their flow across state boundaries are overcome and a period of relatively free trade ensues (Krasner, 1976). In the 19th century, this was the period between 1857 and 1870 when tariff barriers all across Europe were lowered

(Landes, 1969). French prohibition of imported British yarn had led to extensive smuggling as weavers demanded fine cotton and worsted yarns not available on the home market (Clapham, 1966). Napoleon III was convinced by economic liberals and French consumers that open competition would stimulate industrialization. Even the United States lowered its tariffs briefly before the Civil War as the Southern planters and New York merchants attempted to strengthen the economic link with Britain (Foner, 1941).

Similarly, barriers regulating colonial trade are relaxed as the advantages gained from buying cheaply come to outweigh the forces supporting monopoly and protection. Consumers in the periphery have an interest in buying their imports from the core state that sells them most cheaply, and this tends to disrupt the bilateral colonial exchange network. The returns from colonial monopolies lose their relative importance in the overall expansion of the world economy.

The diffusion of technological innovations from the hegemonic core state (Henderson, 1965) and the stimulus to more efficient production resulting from core competition, leads, in combination with the right domestic political conditions, to the expansion of industrial production in other core states and in some semiperipheral states. In the 19th century, these were the United States, Belgium, Germany, and France (Woodruff, 1973). This results in a more even distribution of competitive advantage across the core.

The expansion of production of processed goods in the core causes the demand for raw materials to rise. Raw material production is more dependent on "natural" factors such as climate and the location of natural resources, so its geographical distribution is necessarily more widespread than the production of processed goods. This dependence on natural conditions also slows technological improvement in the production of raw materials relative to that which is possible in production more amenable to reorganization. In addition, the increased accumulation of capital in the core creates an organized labor force demanding higher wages and other amenities. This provides an incentive for capital to utilize cheaper peripheral labor when possible. All these factors expand and intensify the economic exploitation of the periphery.

The evening out of competitive advantage across the core leads to increased competition among producers for access to markets and raw materials. This is expressed within the core by the reemergence of protective tariffs around home markets (Krasner, 1976), and between the core and the periphery in the tightening of colonial monopolies and the expansion of colonial empires to new areas. The core-periphery trade network shifts back toward a more bilateral structure. This new mercantilism and new imperialism occurs at a point in which the overall growth rate of the world-economy slows down and so competition increases and classes utilize state power to maintain shares of a shrinking pie. Each core country becomes locked into its own colonial empire, and trade between core countries declines in importance (Woodruff, 1973).

Colonial expansion and economic penetration of the periphery mutually reinforce one another, although formal colonization is fiscally expensive and is often a defensive (or even preventative) result of core competition over access to peripheral resources and markets (Murray, 1976). The scramble for black Africa which culminated in its division among the imperial powers in 1885 was the result of *anticipatory* economic and political competition.

The period of conflict and disorganization of the world-economy brought about by increasing competition between core states creates room for the emergence of peripheral resistance, as does the increased demand for raw materials, which improves the market position of producers in the periphery. Peripheral independence movements may receive support from core powers in a position to benefit from breaking down the colonial monopolies of other core powers. British support for Spanish American independence movements is a case in point. Decolonization and resistance from the periphery increase the costs of exploitation, and this forces core capital to reconsider the possibilities for more intensive exploitation at home. The creation of formally independent states in the periphery, although their sovereignty is compromised by neocolonial forms of core-periphery domination, nevertheless increases the cost of exploitation. It creates barriers to further colonial expansion (or recolonization), and multi-lateralizes the structure of trade as peripheral states play off core countries against one another. As in the core, however, opposition from one area drives capital to where opposition is less, and this provides the motive force for the continual expansion and deepening of capitalist exploitation.

While this theoretical formulation of the relationship between uneven development in the core and changes in the core-periphery structure needs much more work, it is fruitful to begin thinking about how to test the propositions suggested above. The measurement and analysis of structural variables is always a difficult task, and the problems of comparative analysis on a single case, the modern world-system, are great but not, I think, insurmountable. The attempt to do such analysis, to confront the theoretical notions with formal data, will enable us to refine the formulation. This theoretical and empirical work does not take place in a vacuum. Hopefully, it will provide us with a more useful understanding of capitalist development, its limits, and the transition to socialism.

NOTES

1. I am following Wallerstein's (1974) usage. A core state in the world-system is one in which there is a strong state apparatus, production is diversified, and tends to be composed of highly processed goods produced by skilled, relatively highly paid labor. A peripheral area is characterized by a weak state, an economy specialized in the production of one or two relatively unprocessed goods (raw materials) by unskilled, low-wage (or coerced) labor.

2. A similar process can be seen to operate within federal nation-states. The demise of New York City is a case in point.

3. Rosa Luxemburg (1968), in arguing this thesis, based her case on the contention that the sale of all commodities necessary for expanded reproduction cannot be accomplished within a system composed exclusively of wage labor and capital. For a telling critique of this position, see Bukharin (1976).

REFERENCES

AMIN, S. (1976). Unequal development. New York: Monthly Review Press.
BUKHARIN, N. (1976). Imperialism and the accumulation of capital. New York: Monthly Review Press.
CHASE-DUNN, C.K., and RUBINSON, R. (1976). "Toward a structural perspective on the world-system." Paper delivered at the World Systems Seminar sponsored by the American Academy of Arts and Sciences, Stanford University, April.
CLAPMAN, J.H. (1966). Economic development of France and Germany. Cambridge: Cambridge University Press.
EMMANUEL, A. (1972). Unequal exchange: A study of the imperialism of trade. New York: Monthly Review Press.
FONER, P. (1941). Business and slavery: The New York merchants and the irrepressible conflict. Chapel Hill: University of North Carolina Press.
HENDERSON, W.D. (1965). Britain and industrial Europe: Studies in British influence on the Industrial Revolution in Western Europe, 1750-1870. London: Leicester University Press.
HOBSBAWM, E.J. (1968). Industry and empire. Baltimore: Penquin.
KRASNER, S.D. (1976). "State power and the structure of international trade." World Politics, 28(3):317-347.
LANDES, D. (1969). The unbound Prometheus. Cambridge: Cambridge University Press.
LUXEMBURG, R. (1968). The accumulation of capital. New York: Monthly Review Press.
MANDEL, E. (1975). Late capitalism. London: New Left Books.
MARX, K. (1967). Capital I, III. New York: International Publishers.
MURRAY, M. (1976). "Capitalist expansion and the colonial system." Paper delivered at the annual meetings of the American Sociological Association, New York.
POLANYI, K. (1944). The great transformation. Boston: Beacon.
POULANTZAS, N. (1975). Classes in contemporary capitalism. London: New Left Books.
ROBINSON, R. and GALLAGHER, J. (1953). "The imperialism of free trade." Economic History Review, 6(1):1-15.
SZYMANSKI, A. (1973). "Military spending and economic stagnation." American Journal of Sociology, 79(1):1-14.
WALLERSTEIN, I. (1974). The modern world-system, Vol. I, Capitalist agriculture and the origins of the European world-economy in the sixteenth century. New York: Academic Press.

———— (forthcoming). "Dutch hegemony in the 17th century world-economy." Chapter
    2 in The modern world-system, Vol. 2.
WILSON, C.H. (1957). Profit and power: A study of England and the Dutch Wars.
    London: Longmans.
WOODRUFF, W. (1973). "The emergence of an international economy 1700-1914."
    In C.M. Cipollo (ed.), Fontana economic history of Europe: The emergence of
    industrial societies, Part 2. New York: Franklin Watts.

Chapter 7

CONTINUITY, CHANGE, AND TENSION IN GLOBAL CAPITALISM

Douglas Dowd

I

Radicals, especially those who see themselves as Marxists, rightly deplore and condemn the narrowness, the shallowness, and the smugness of mainstream social analysis—ahistorical, watertight compartments of "theory" or "fact" floating on the here and now, buoyed by the warm air of ideal constructs, neglecting the origins, the connections, and the human meaning of social relations. Neither able nor inclined to distinguish between the fundamental and the trivial in the social process, their yield is some combination of obfuscation and whitewash.

But if we are to have the right to mutter contemptuous imprecations at such "social science," it will be because we are ourselves attempting the essential work thus implied: endless historical study, guided by and continually shaping social theory, reaching back in time and out in space, cutting through diverse social formations. What we cannot do is to assume that the major part of our work has been done for us by the genius of Marx and Engels, and/or of Lenin; we should not be candidates for Engels's jibe that "the materialist conception of history also has a lot of friends nowadays to whom it serves as an excuse for *not* studying history."

One place to begin, in seeking to show just how much work remains to be done by us, is to ask how much of what we need to know Marx *could* have done, and how much and what he *sought* to do. Like all mortals, Marx was caught up in the inherent impossibility of fully understanding the social system of his own time; that impossibility resides in the very nature of the social process. What is remarkable was Marx's ability to cut through the fatty tissue to the muscle and the nerve structure of the capitalist system. Unlike everyone else, Marx was able to discover the *essential* characteristics of that system's political economy: its dependence upon and its ability to exploit, to accumulate (that is, to expand), and to be ruled oligarchically.

Marx took Great Britain as his empirical focus for *Capital*. As he studied and wrote, however, even in Britain capitalism was only beginning to appear in some full-blown form. Reminding ourselves of that, we must also note that in those same years capitalism in Britain and elsewhere was also beginning to move away from its mid-19th century forms—by today's standards, a primitive technology and simple forms of business, political and social organization.

What do we find when we ask what Marx was and was not *trying* to do in *Capital*, both his most influential and his most systematic treatise? Marx was a theorist, and the economic theory of *Capital* is highly abstract, as was entirely appropriate, for in it Marx was seeking to respond dialectically to the abstract economic theory of his day. He did not seek to bring together the entirety of the operating characteristics of capitalist political economy (to say nothing of capitalist *society*, or the *global* economy). He was "merely" seeking to show: (1) that the classical political economists had not explained the existence of the most vital form of income in their own theoretical system, namely, profit; (2) that using their labor theory of value, but doing so with logical consistency and clarity, "proved" the dependence of the capitalist system upon labor exploitation; and (3) that the system, thus, could and also must move through time in a process of sustained capital accumulation. Marx went on from that to posit, however, (4) that the "contradictions" inherent to such a system would provide an intermittently weak accumulation process and an ever stronger, more conscious, better organized, and ultimately revolutionary working-class movement that would seize the opportunity provided by crisis to transform and transcend the capitalist system.

All that may be seen as a stupendous intellectual achievement in its own time and still for ours, and yet we must insist that it was not enough for Marx's time, for ensuing decades, or, most especially, for now and tomorrow. What I seek to move to here is this: one may study the collected works of Marx and Engels and never comprehend the resiliency and the stamina that have marked the capitalist process from their day down to ours. If it remains extraordinary that the essential needs of capitalism in Marx's day, as he saw them, are just as essential today and that therefore (for that among other reasons) *any* understanding of capitalism must begin with Marxism, it is of equal importance to state that the Marxism of the past and of the present leaves us in a recurring state of surprise at the extraordinary career of capitalism, and not least at its staying power—despite hell and high water.

In what follows, I shall argue that the "hell and high water" that capitalism has survived (and which it also created, of course) may be seen as having made possible and as having required substantial social changes which—in the absence of effective revolutionary forces—have acted to strengthen, not to weaken, the ability of the system to meet its essential needs and for those who preside over it to realize their aims of profit and power. Put differently, what Marxists see as the "contradictions" of capitalism have, in their consequences, been the source and the stimulus more of its staying power than of its downfall, and have, in practice, *prevented* its downfall.

Another consequence of the latter developments has been to keep the Left in the advanced countries weak and off balance—a condition worsened by the tendency of the Left to view the sociohistorical and thus also the political economic elements of the capitalist process narrowly, oversimply, mechanically—in a word, nondialectically. The upsurge of Marxian self-criticism of recent years, of which this conference is both a result and an instance, is, one may hope, taking us to a sounder and safer analytical position. If so, our politics may also take a turn for the better.

II

I should like to look further at the notion of "contradiction" before proceeding. Like so many important concepts and arguments in the Marxian lexicon, this term is a metaphor: as such, of course, it can be no more than suggestive. Unfortunately, and as has frequently happened with others of Marx's brilliant metaphors, the notion of "contradiction" has too often been taken literally; it then becomes a barrier to understanding, for thus seen it implies some sort of unyielding, absolute opposition among social relations and forces, rather than the fluid, dialectical process Marx must have had in mind.[1] I wish to connect such misleading interpretations of this basic concept (and therefore of much else) with what I take to be *one* of the reasons for the undeveloped state of Marxian social analysis. This will lead me to examine certain aspects of capitalist history in ways stimulated by Wallerstein (1974), wherein I shall try to show how the weakness or the strength of the accumulation process has allowed "contradictions" to generate destructive or to yield therapeutic social changes.

"The primary contradiction" of capitalism, as Marx saw it, is between the *social* nature of production and the *private* nature of appropriation. This, in turn, is the source of numerous other lesser "contradictions" which, taken together, produce both the intermittent crises and conflicts of the capitalist process and, as well, its final overthrow. However, it seems equally clear that the energy, the dynamism, the vitality, and, in general, the positive aspects of the capitalist process also arise out of these same "contradictions"; the source of life and of death are one and the same.

Thus, and by way of example, what produces the probability of "overproduction" or of "underconsumption" is, of course, essential for the very possibility of capital accumulation, profitability, and technological advance of capitalism itself; or, on a different level, the forces that bring competition to an end are quite the same as those creating monopoly. And, although monopoly has a bad name among both conventional and Marxian economists (who, more often than not, have seen it as a "fetter" upon the capitalist process), it seems instead that all those developments that monopoly makes possible and requires, in their confluence after World War II as monopoly capitalism, have given the system its strongest lease on life. If that lease seems once more to be expiring, it will be wise for us to ask what the present deepening of capitalism's "contradictions" might yield in the way of new stays of execution, while also busying ourselves to prevent those ways from being developed.

It is a commonplace that crisis—another metaphor—is a condition (or, better, a process) combining threat with opportunity. In the context of capitalist development, crisis, which arises out of contradictions, occurs as the omnipresent strains, conflicts, inequities, and dislocations of the capitalist process push through the social surface, allowed and caused to do so by the weakening of the protective membrane of that system— its accumulation process. Thus is produced a broader and deeper set of social tensions, the resolution of which requires substantial social change—the required and possible degrees of which, it may be asserted, have become increasingly more substantial over time.

What is *required*, in Marxian analysis, must always be seen as what is made possible. What is required and facilitated by capitalist crises is *change*. And it should never be forgotten that capitalism, more than any other social system, not only produces social change but *thrives* on it. Schumpeter (1942) saw some of this when he characterized the processes of technological change as "gales of creative destruction." Fred Block (1977) sees another part of it when he argues that "class struggle is responsible for much of the economic dynamism of capitalism."

From this hasty setting of the stage, I now move to the main purpose of the paper, an attempt to sketch out historical support for the notion that the inevitable tensions and disasters (economic, military, social, etc.) of capitalist development have—once more in the absence of effective revolutionary forces—directly and indirectly yielded those vast social changes which, in turn, have been the indispensable means by which the essential needs of the system continue to be met: its needs for ever widening realms of exploitation, for continuous expansion, and for concentrated rule.

III

Clearly, the approach suggested by the foregoing remarks has been at least partially stimulated by Wallerstein's "world-system" analysis. His emphasis on the complexities attending the birth and the early life of capitalism (e.g., the "tiers" of core, semi-periphery, and periphery, the "variegated" systems of labor control, and the diverse state machineries) points to an underlying pattern of substantially still *greater* complexity in all these respects. It also requires one to think through the bewildering manner in which the various dimensions of all that would interact over time and space. Such complexity could not but yield a process of not only constant but essentially uncontrollable change. Not only uncontrollable, however; also considerably less dangerous to the basic system. The greater the number of variables, the less likely that any conflict could endure or deepen, when all the variables are in a process of continuous interaction and change. The head-on, fight-to-the-finish conflict, suggested by the literal interpretation of contradiction as absolute opposition, becomes most unlikely; the social process is too slippery.

The perspective Wallerstein provides is one of conflict, unevenness, turbulence, and confusion as among the hardiest of allies for the vital process of expansion in the birth process of capitalism:

> The ability to expand successfully is a function both of the ability to maintain relative social solidarity at home (in turn a function of the mechanisms of the distribution of reward) and the arrangements that can be made to use *cheap* labor *far away*.... Expansion also involves unequal development and therefore differential rewards, and unequal development in a multilayered format of layers within layers, each one polarized in terms of a bimodal distribution of rewards. Thus, concretely, in the sixteenth century, there was the differential of the core of the European world-economy versus its peripheral areas, within the European core between states, within states between regions and strata, within regions between city and country, and ultimately within more local units. The solidarity of the system was based ultimately on this phenomenon of unequal development, since the multilayered complexity provided the possibility of multilayered identification and the constant realignment of political forces, which provided at one and the same time the underlying turbulence that permitted technological development and political transformations, and also the ideological confusion that contained the rebellions, whether they were rebellions of slowdown, of force, or of flight. [Wallerstein, 1974:85-86; italics in original]

All that was in Wallerstein's "sixteenth century"—i.e., 1450-1640. What of the capitalist process of the past century or so, roughly from Marx's time to ours? That process has been *more* complex in structure, *more* solidaristic in the core countries, *more* turbulent, characterized *more* by rapid technological and political developments, and it has been awash in ideological "confusion." But not continuously, of course; it also had an agonized mid-period, much of the first half of the 20th century. Those decades, as the most perilous and the most violent in capitalism's history, reveal that rapid change and turmoil by themselves tell us nothing; we must attend to the content of the processes of change. It will help us to understand the ways in which "contradiction" and consequent changes strengthen capitalism, if we examine the period and the changes which came closest to killing it off.

IV

In order to do that, we should look first at the immediately preceding decades, the last half of the 19th century. It is the period viewed nostalgically by most conventional economic historians as a "golden age." In what were or were shortly to become the leading powers of the globe, industrialism, capitalism, and nationalism, all feeding upon each other, took on increased and greater strength—all the while requiring and fueling the imperialist scramble. It was a period of unprecedentedly rapid, deep, and pervasive change of all sorts for almost all societies—large and small, powerful and weak, imperialist and imperialized: destructive of the traditional societies still remaining, powerfully strengthening for the modern societies of the core countries. But not for long.

Already by the first years of the 20th century, shock waves of resistance to further changes of one sort had begun to build up, while other kinds of changes were encouraged and hastened. It was those of the latter sort that at least temporarily felled the system thereafter. What was needed for the continuous and smooth functioning of global capitalism was an accelerated process of capital accumulation, in turn requiring the deepening, the broadening, and the further integration of markets among and between the countries of the entire globe. What happened instead were increasing, and increasingly abrasive, attempts to hold others at bay, on the one hand, and to take over markets and territories already controlled, on the other. The growth of the pie could not keep up with the growth of appetites; the stench of war was around the corner.

What prompted both kinds of changes was the slowing down of the global accumulation process, capitalism's fatal disease. The golden age had taken its lustre from the super-charged process of combined economic and geographic expansion, enabling and depending upon what has usefully been called "the second industrial revolution"—the new era of cheap transportation and communications, of cheap foodstuffs, of cheap metals and fuels, and of cheap machinery—and, thus, the dawn of our era of mass-produced capital and consumer goods and, of course, of pervasive monopoly. All this just as Volume I of *Capital* was, so to speak, in press. It was in those very decades, from the 1860s onward, that the capitalist system functioned most smoothly in its global form, when the national capitalisms of the world were best nourished by the "global division of labor." But the process was, of course, rife with "contradictions."

The rapidity and the spread of the industrialization process was much stimulated by the rivalrous national states, each seeking to stretch and to strengthen its muscles. Each sought to be a full and powerful industrial state; the predictable result was a dangerous duplication of productive structures. Each industrializing nation sought, and had to seek, not only strong trading relations with the other major powers—then as now, each other's major markets—but also markets, resources, strategic locations, and investment outlets in the colonial world. The race was sharply limited in time, for the surface of the globe is fixed; most of it, as the race warmed up, was already occupied. Global capitalism thus moved rapidly toward a massive "realization crisis"—that is, toward depression—but arrived at war first.

The changes which had integrated and thus strengthened the national capitalist economies now were replaced, increasingly and inexorably, by those which set them harshly against each other by changes which, prompted by an inadequate accumulation process, further weakened that process. For the calamity of World War I to occur, no further stimulus was necessary.

It could be argued that the pre-World War I accumulation process had to end when and how it did, without further qualification. But it is necessary to point to an additional and less obvious "contradiction" central to the entire process. Whatever may have been required in earlier times, by the mid-19th century a dynamic accumulation process required the clear domination of one relative superpower. In no other way could the process find the discipline it needed, given the aggressive tendencies of the many nations party to it, nor could it find the needed capital. Britain was the superpower, and it exercised the required discipline through its great financial strength. That all the nations involved were capitalist nations meant that an unavoidable result of the industrialization process would be the duplicative productive structures noted earlier, with the looming threat of excess capacity, of deadly competition for markets and resources; that the processes were strong and pervasive meant, in practice, that Great Britain's relative dominance and the dependence upon it must steadily diminish and finally vanish, thus to unleash the underlying forces of international anarchy. After 1870, the world economy appeared as a rich man's club; after 1910, and for more than a generation, the reality became that of gang warfare in the streets.

Thus, it may be posited that the role of a ruling class—providing direction and control—within a national economy has its essential counterpart in the role played by a dominant nation in the global capitalist economy. That role, provided by Britain into the 20th century, could not be continued when its relative superiority began to fade. During the war and throughout the interwar period, the U.S., for a variety of reasons, could not and did not adopt that role when, super-ficially viewed, it might have. The U.S. could and had to bring order to global capitalism after World War II, if capitalism was to revive and flourish. Of which, more later.

That global capitalism did not perish during those bent and bloody years was due not so much to its resiliency during the period, although it had some, but was due more to the absence of any significant alternative having been posed—unless fascism (as it should not be) is seen as that alternative. Even in the long years of deep and violent crisis, whole decades in which capitalism was unable either to meet its own economic and political standards or to avoid massive internecine warfare, the Left developed neither the analysis nor the politics to gain (or to deserve?) effective popular support, let alone to mount a revolutionary movement anywhere but in Russia, which surely is the exception proving the rule. Will future crises produce a better effort from the Left in the advanced capitalist societies? There are some reasons for thinking so; but it also seems that the capitalist state will be better able to stave off anything as severe or as prolonged as the decades after 1910 and, if anything, be better able to confront and to mani-pulate crisis to its advantage in the future than in the past. If that is so, it is because of what has been learned through practice, the hard way, as capitalism was allowed to survive what should have been the fatal challenges of its "contradic-tions" in the first half of this century. Having done so, like tempered steel, it is probably sturdier than ever.

V

Surely, if Marx and Engels's expectations are to be taken seriously, capitalism should have been overthrown in the leading countries some time early in this century. That it has not been and that its prospects for surviving the entire century seem at the moment to be something more than merely finite does not reflect badly upon Marxism as a method. It does suggest, of course, that the method requires more careful, diligent, and imaginative application than it has yet received.

Marx himself emphasized, but did not systematically examine, the breadth and the complexity of the conditions surrounding capitalism's birth pangs, its period of "primitive accumulation." But one does not get from Marx, as one does from Anderson (1974) and Wallerstein, a sense of the precariousness of either the birth or the infancy of the new system. One cannot read Anderson's forceful historical analysis without perceiving that the very genesis of capitalism was an improbability, made possible only by its vital umbilical connection with the *unique* features of *Western* European feudalism, *and* by what he calls "the collision and coalescence" (and lasting impact) of Roman and Germanic institutions.[2]

Anderson is a Marxist, of course, but his analysis is scarcely in keeping with the oft-assumed "universal stages" from "ancient, to feudal, to bourgeois" (and to socialist?) society, able and likely to happen for all and everywhere, if at different times and rates of change. And, of course, Wallerstein, in emphasizing the complex process of the period of "primitive accumulation" may be read also as insisting upon the great delicacy of the balance and interaction between economic, political, social, cultural, technological, and geographic relations which, in anything but an inevitable outcome, laid the foundations for what, by the late 18th century, had perhaps become an irresistible global rush.

Marx appears to have taken both the birth and the early strengths of capitalism too much for granted, as well he might have, given the focus of *Capital* (if not, however, of his other works). Is it not true, and for the same reasons, that he seems to have underestimated capitalism's later strengths, and its ability to find ways to endure?

In analyzing "the economic laws of motion of capitalist society," and finding the "primary contradiction" within that sphere, Marx—understandably for him, but much less so for subsequent Marxists—did not anticipate that the capitalist process would respond to the deepening of that "contradiction" by spreading it beyond the "economy" and into every nook and cranny of society, just as he did not analyze the probable meaning of Western capitalism spreading into every nook and cranny of the globe. The former process, the "socialization" of capitalism, was neither necessary nor possible in Marx's day; the latter, imperialism in its modern forms, was just then getting underway. Some elaboration is in order.

"The primary contradiction" of capitalism lies in the social relations and processes of *production*, and it is from that same sphere that crisis, class consciousness, and the "ultimate" undoing of capitalism are presumed to emerge. For the mid-quarters of the 19th century, and especially in the conditions of laissez-faire British capitalism, Marx's analysis has a strong ring of plausibility. But British capitalism was exceptional in its sociopolitical as well as in its economic conditions, and able to be so in critical part because it was *first* in the industrial capitalist race. Even British capitalism, though, like French, German, Italian, Japanese, and U.S. capitalism, had by the first years of this century begun to wobble and lurch *toward* what global industrial capitalism required for its survival, but which it could not and did not achieve until after World War II: the socio-political-cultural-economic-military-geographic complex now called monopoly capitalism.

The severe problem posed for a sustained accumulation process by the "social nature of production and the private nature of appropriation" (and exacerbated by competitive nationalism) has been rendered manageable by the increasingly social (and international) nature of appropriation. The "market" of Marx's day was almost totally private, though, of course, global—if thinly so, by comparison with today. Its main dynamic was in the capital goods sector, with some useful support from exported light consumer goods. That private market has now been "socialized" (but not made socialist, of course) through the manifold taxing, spending, and shaping activities of the many-sided and massive capitalist state; it has been internationalized and Americanized in ways and to degrees that make it qualitatively different from and stronger by far than the British-dominated "world economy" of the 19th century; and all its economic and geographic sectors have been reconstructed, modernized, integrated, and strengthened by a surprisingly sophisticated U.S. since World War II. If all that were not enough to breathe new life into the system, the evermore alienating processes of work in particular (as Braverman, 1974, has shown so well) and of everyday life in general, have in their turn provided dynamic support for one further and essential requirement and possibility of advanced capitalism, namely, media manipulated consumerism and its underbelly, media manipulated politics.

In this complex process, reluctantly forced upon a largely protesting capitalist class, what can be seen as "deepening contradictions" have not only been rendered relatively harmless, but very useful, as they have been spread throughout the society and over the globe and thus "shallowed." The process of rule has become more diffuse through such changes, but it has not taken from capital what it needs and prizes most: profits and power. The era of monopoly capitalism, that is, the years since World War II, have provided more of both than ever before, and that to the shrinking number of capitalists who have created and survived the also essential centralization processes of advanced capitalism. Despite and because of the system's troubles of this century, they have never had it so good.

VI

Up to here, I have focused upon the ability of the capitalist system to survive due to actions taken at the top—whether arising out of harsh circumstance, fear, and opposition, or from opportunities perceived. The rulers of the system have been able to twist and to turn in response to what could have become deadly developments; in doing so, they have learned not only how to survive but to flourish. Their ability to do all this has come not only from their possession of basic power over life and death, but also from their social authority, what Gramsci (1971) called their ideological "hegemony." And, of course, their survival has depended in critical part upon the absence of any effective challenge from socialist revolutionary forces in the advanced countries. Now it is time to attempt a brief analysis from the bottom up, to see why revolutionary developments have been absent, and to speculate briefly on prospects for the future.

Had there been an effective revolutionary force in any one or more of the advanced capitalist countries, surely its substantial center would have been, as Marx thought, the industrial working class. I believe much of what we have to understand about why that did not occur has been put together by Paul Sweezy in his 1967 essay commemorating the 100th anniversary of Volume I of *Capital*. I shall try not to distort his views in the compressed version that follows: The proletariat Marx had in mind was that of the mid-19th century. Industrial workers then were forced by their own powerlessness and by the technology of the time to work at mind- and body-numbing tasks, and to do so under conditions that not only threw workers together in increasing numbers, but also in essentially homogeneous conditions. This was a very different process from that preceding the era of the industrial revolution (the era of "petty commodity production"), and very different also from the contemporary conditions of the working class in advanced industrial capitalist countries. As Sweezy (1967:37-38) says,

In terms of the occupational composition of the labor force, then, the two chief consequences of modern industry's revolutionary technology have been 1) a drastic (and continuing)

reduction in the production-worker component, and 2) a vast proliferation of job categories in the distribution and service sectors of the economy. At the same time there has taken place a slow but cumulatively substantial increase in the real wages of both production and non-production workers. In part this reflects an increase in the cost of production of labor power as the educational and training requirements of the new employment categories have risen. And in part it reflects the fact that the workers—and here we mean primarily production workers— have been able through non-revolutionary class struggle to wrest from the capitalists a part of the fruits of increasing productivity.

Marx did not argue that workers in the era of petty commodity production were or should have been "revolutionary." It is doubtful that he would have believed they "should be" revolutionary in the conditions within today's advanced countries. In short, there was a period—say, the last half of the 19th century and up to World War I—in the early part of which the industrial working class had every reason to be impelled toward revolution. By its later part, and most especially because of the combined impact of imperialism and rising real wages, those reasons had diminished. That capitalism in the advanced countries was able to persist through that most precarious period meant that it would also find its way into a future in which, if there was any threat to its power, it would not come principally from the working class in the advanced countries.

But Sweezy and we may ask a different question:

Does the fact that capitalism in Western Europe and North America survived the initial period of modern industry and that its new technology then went on progressively to reduce the revolutionary potential of the proletariat, mean that as of the second half of the 20th century we have to abandon the whole idea of a revolutionary agent destined to overthrow the capitalist order? [Sweezy, 1967:39]

It does not mean that. Just as the functioning of the system
has been and must be global, it is also true that its strains and
conflicts are global in sweep. The "world-system" approach
of Wallerstein, his own substantial elaboration and systematic
analysis of Marx's occasional observations, was anticipated
by Sweezy, when he said,

> Once it is recognized that capitalism is not and never has
> been confined to one or more industrializing countries, but is
> rather a global system embracing both the (relatively few)
> industrializing countries and their (relatively numerous)
> satellites and dependencies, it becomes quite clear that the
> future of the system cannot be adequately analyzed in terms
> of the forces at work in any part of the system but must take
> full account of the *modus operandi* of the system as a whole.
> [Sweezy, 1967:40]

Especially is this true when we turn our attention once
more to the vital role played by the accumulation process in
maintaining not only capitalist prosperity but capitalist peace.
The ability of the capitalist process to immobilize the revolutionary potential of the industrial working class has depended
more on the stick in its early years and more on the carrot as
we approach the present. The carrots have come not only
from the advancing technology of the advanced countries, but
also from the ever-spreading and deepening exploitation of the
peoples of the Third World. This is not the place to enable
an adequate argument, but it may be asserted here that there
is no reasonable likelihood that the benefits of the accumula-
tion/technological process can *ever* be spread among the
peoples of the Third World either in the time period or to
the degree achieved in the advanced countries. It may be
asserted further that the advanced countries are themselves
faced by what appears to be a foreseeable future of intractable
"stagflation," and what has come to be called "reduced
expectations." All that, in association with the spreading
and deepening of malaise, skepticism, disgust, and fear

concerning the normal functioning of this system—whose functioning as an economy has now and necessarily spread like an oil stain into all the cracks and sectors of our lives— is likely to increase the difficulties of rule. It is likely, in different words, to cause rule to return increasingly to the stick.

That does not guarantee the emergence of revolutionary forces either in the Third World or ours; nothing ever has. It does mean that we, like the capitalists, need not give up hope; it means that we have the time to make the effort to teach, to learn, to organize, and to struggle against what has never been omnipotent, but has always been powerful; and for what has never been assured, but has always been possible.

NOTES

1. Raymond Williams (1973) provides a lucid and useful discussion of this problem as it affects an equally important metaphor in Marxism.

2. Both volumes by Perry Anderson should be read, perhaps best so after reading the gist of his position in the Conclusions put forth in *Lineages of the Absolute State*.

REFERENCES

ANDERSON, P. (1974a). Passages from antiquity to feudalism. London: NLB.
——— (1974b). Lineages of the absolute state. London: NLB.
BLOCK, F. (1977). "The ruling class does not rule: Notes on the Marxist theory of the state." Socialist Revolution, 33(May-June):21.
BRAVERMAN, H. (1974). Labor and monopoly capital. New York: Monthly Review Press.
GRAMSCI, A. (1971). Pp. 206-275 in Q. Hoare and G.N. Smith (eds.), Selections from the prison notebooks. New York: International.
SCHUMPETER, J.A. (1942). Capitalism, socialism, and democracy. New York: Harper and Row.
SWEEZY, P. (1967). "Marx and the proletariat." Monthly Review, (December): 37-38.

WALLERSTEIN, I. (1974). The modern world-system: Capitalist agriculture and the origins of the European world-economy in the sixteenth century. New York: Academic Press.

WILLIAMS, R. (1973). "Base and superstructure in Marxist cultural theory." New Left Review, (November-December).

PART 4

WORLD SYSTEM ANALYSIS:
THEORETICAL AND METHODOLOGICAL ISSUES

Chapter 8

WORLD-SYSTEM ANALYSIS: METHODOLOGICAL ISSUES

Terence Hopkins

The topic is methodological issues. It is a brave one to attempt to address. I shall try to do so in two steps. After some preliminary observations, I shall try to speak to what I think are three issues under the general heading of concept formation and measurement. Then I shall speak on two or three under the heading of explanation and interpretation. I take it that the issues concern the study of long-term large-scale change—in that sense, historical transformations—and that the job of someone commenting methodologically on such work is to raise questions not about *what* we think in the course of this work but about *how* we think as we proceed. I shall try to do that. What I have to say will thus inevitably be distant from the kind of discourse we have been having. My apologies in advance.

I would like to pose an opening query which I cannot answer, but which I think any adequate methodological discussion would have to address: Why are these matters up for discussion? Why do we have the kinds of issues we have? What is our intellectual world—in that sense, our consciousness—which leads us to be concerned, now, with these kinds of discussions? I cannot answer these questions, but I believe an adequate epistemology would at least address them.

That kind of question it seems to me raises additional ones about our understanding of inquiry. Ours is academic inquiry; this is an academic conference. There are therefore severe limitations on the kinds of queries that can be addressed and on the criteria of adequacy that can be appropriately used. I think we have a very deep need to put in front of us how we are, in fact, thinking. Because we come out of particular settings, we have learned particular ways to think, and it is not at all obvious that they are the most useful ones for our work. I think we need a lot of help here, from one another, from others, in trying to visualize the changing shape of the intellectual terrain we perforce work in.

CONCEPTS AND CONCEPTUALIZATION

Forcing ourselves to think in ways we are not used to. . . . Here let me turn to the first of the broad headings, concept formation and measurement. Those familiar with the analytical-philosophical headings of the 1950s and 1960s will recognize this one. There are three subjects I wish to deal with, three movements I think we perform in the course of inquiry into long-term large-scale change.

For the first I will use the expression "movement from the abstract to the concrete." One general form of this movement is from concept (abstract) to indicator (concrete). I think the concept-indicator "movement of thought" is so ingrained in our understanding of inquiry that it takes an act of will not to proceed straight off in that fashion. The format is reasonably clear; there are marvelous descriptions of it; it is an important way of thinking, a very important way. I think Lazarsfeld, in every third publication on methodological matters, goes into the movement from formulation of a concept through to associated ideas through to selection of indicators through to their combination into indices and so forth. More abstractly there is the Hempel-like formulation, the imagery of a theory as a network of substantive concepts (nodes) and logical relations between them (threads), floating, as it were, above a world of reality to which the theory is linked by "rules of interpretation"; the rules tell one how to descend from the concepts to the observations that indicate or measure the concepts and how to ascend from observations by conceptualizing, interpreting them. The movement here is analogous, then, to the movement in a relation of logical inclusion, from abstract concept via successive additions of specifics or attributes to the concrete, the "real indicators"; from the concrete via the dropping of these attributes, to the abstract. That is one sense of this movement.

There is a very different form of the movement which is analogous not to inclusion-relations but to part-whole relations. In this case, the part (a theoretical process) is the abstract, the whole is the concrete. Concrete here is a level of conceptualization, it is not the "real world." This sense of the movement from abstract to concrete is the one Marx discusses in his very brief and elliptical remarks on "The Method of Political Economy." As a methodological directive, it is extremely demanding. Consider, as an abstract formulation, the reproduction cycle (basically the array of arguments set forth in Volume I of *Capital*) and take the concept "capital accumulation"—how do you proceed from there? Well, if you work with the notion of the concept-indicator interpretation of abstract-concrete, you have one set of directions. You are to begin looking for indicators of degree-of or amount-of capital accumulation at some place(s) in some period(s), presuming there are ways of measuring it straight off, more or less validly, more or less reliably. The part-whole directive gives one an utterly different set of directions. It says to keep moving out by successive determinations, bringing in successive parts—themselves abstract processes—in continuous juxtaposition and in this way form the whole which you need for interpreting and explaining the historical changes or conditions under examination. I will come back to this later, when I take up some topics under the heading of explanation-interpretation.

Now, in this context, I have difficulties with, for example, Theda Skocpol's and Kay Trimberger's notion of revolutions, because I sense that the term is used as a category ("abstract") into which events ("concrete") can be classified. And I have doubts about proceeding that way in the kind of work we do. Revolutionary transformations of social relations—of production and, thus, of all others—seem to me very abstract "parts" (theoretical processes) which have to brought into successive relation with other "parts" (other theoretical processes) in order to move toward the concrete. That is *still* a conceptualization (or an interpretation-sketch); but then, in the fullness of the whole so formed, one "interprets" observational statements; or, alternatively, one "measures" selected and partial "outcomes" of the complex of processes.

I guess I have similar difficulties, therefore, with Walter Goldfrank's "fascism." If it is just a condition, an attribute of a regime, it is not very interesting. *If* it is a theoretical process (a part) dealing with rule and therefore relational, I need to know far more about the movement he takes in going from the abstract to the concrete, toward a fuller whole, and within that, from observational statements (about "German rearmament") to the now-formed social whole in which the "rearmament" has meaning, from which it derives meaning. That is one topic under this heading.

A second concern and movement is quite different. It has to do with our locating ourselves "in time" in relation to our subject matter. One notion of time is that it is an objective time scale—it is "out there," forming a coordinate of our observations and ourselves. We can position ourselves and our subject matter—it is in the past, it is going to be in the future, so many years, and so forth—and so fix our respective places. This has the great advantage that we can always undo the relation so formed; we can shift ourselves about, in the way anthropologists do when writing in "the ethnographic present," which of course simply eliminates the real relations between the researcher and the researched.

I do not think the world system perspective, as it is developing and as we begin to reread and reunderstand matters from this angle of vision, permits this. I think the perspective we are trying to develop premises a multi-level, complex system of social action that is comprehensive and singular not only in scope—and so forms a spatial "world" with its own changing geopolitical boundaries—but also in time—and so forms a temporal "world" with its own irreversible sequences and nonarbitrary periodicities. It forms, that is, a single temporal, developing world, through its deepening synchronization, its chronologically ordered thrust, its cycles of expansion and contraction, and its secular trends.

This is not a concept that is easy to grasp or to work with. Most of us do not consider "time" in this sense as an integral dimension of the systems we predicate and examine and, *inseparately,* of predicating and examining them. Instead, we think of it, as I indicated, as an independently given ordering dimension in terms of which we make and array observations bearing on the systems we are examining. The modern world system, however, cannot be usefully thought of as analogous to a racing car that is "started" and then "timed" over the course it ran and continues to run. As we conceive it, it does not function so much *over* time as *through* time. Time in the form of its trends and cycles is, like space, constitutive of it as a system, not merely a coordinate of its properties' variations. It does not have a history or set of histories so much as it constitutes a history or set of histories.

Now, that is obviously a difficult epistemological premise, but if we can grant it for now, we can see that we are strictly limited in the ways in which we may form working concepts. We cannot proceed, as Weber did, in sketching the dimensions, features, and aspects of, for example, the social relations of domination—that is, bureaucracy—to pull out an attribute from here, an attribute from there, an attribute from somewhere else, and form with them an "ideal-type" construct. That way of proceeding is precisely to deny a central feature of what we are trying to study and a central premise of how we are trying to study it. Or maybe a better example. We cannot construct a typology of the social aspects of the division of labor, as Weber did in those marvelous sections/15-24a of the second chapter of *Economy and Society*, where he takes up just about all of the distinctions any of us might imagine. For, as he says, he took most of the ideas from Bücher *except* their formulation as integral to definite historical developments. Instead, if we want to use the ideas, we have to use them in the form in which Bücher presents them, as cumulating *processes* of division of labor in their historical sequences, so that the understanding of something called "division of labor" is as a set of processes, *not* as a set of conditions. Bücher depicts an overall developmental movement carried forward by one major form of the process, then a second one, with the first still going on, then a third form, all intersecting, and so on. He gets to five forms of division of labor as process. I am sure we will be able to find more or maybe collapse some, but the point here is that the concept is itself time-developmental or "historical." Also, and in a different vein, there is Lenin's review in *State and Revolution* of the formulations of the state, in the sense of post-seizure of state power, in Marx and Engels's changing understanding of it as they were analyzing first the 1850s then the 1870s. Something along these lines seems to be to be necessary if we are to build up and to deepen the kinds of concepts we need in order to apprehend the kinds of real movements we seek to analyze and interpret.

The third mental movement in this area that I wish to discuss I will introduce with an analogy. (The exposition here, I might insert, will run on a bit.) I have in mind the figure-ground movement where if one refocuses, what was figure becomes ground and when one refocuses again, what was ground becomes figure. For us, the figure-ground movement seems to take place centrally between social relations and agencies of action, between role and role relation. I think the methodological directive with which we work is that our acting units or agencies can only be thought of as *formed*, and continually reformed, by the relations between them. Perversely, we often think of the relations as only going between the end points, the units or the acting agencies, as if the latter made the relations instead of the relations making the units. Relations, generally, are our figures and acting agencies are our backgrounds. At certain points in conducting analyses, it is of course indispensable to shift about and focus on acting agencies; but I think we too often forget what we have done and fail to shift the focus back again. Let me give here one formal illustration of what I mean and then two of a more substantive sort.

We often address ourselves in inquiry to conditions we call "distributions." One has a set of, say, households, and each exhibits more or less of some condition, say, material well-being, so that we can then say the condition is unequally distributed over the households. We then usually ask questions like "How come?" "What produced the inequality?" "What are the effects?" I think we commonly forget that the directives we work with tell us to envision these distributions as "produced by" the relations among the units, i.e., as themselves merely the totals rows or columns of relational matrices (in the common formats we are used to: input-output tables, who-to-whom interaction summaries, origin-destination arrays, etc.). The same units are arrayed horizontally and vertically, and the resulting cells give the formal locus of their respective dyadic relations, i.e., the formal locus of the ongoing processes. The totals rows and columns, which one literally obtains by some summing operation across rows or down columns, are the "distributions." And so, when we address ourselves to distributions without remembering to see them as summaries of conditions continually resulting from processes among the units, we give up our central focus on relations and perforce become eclectic and ad hoc in our efforts to set forth coherent accounts of "distributions."

Let me give a substantive example. In Chapter Two of *Development of Capitalism*, Lenin addresses himself to a matter then under debate in Russian intellectual circles: "Why was there increasing inequality among the peasants? Why were some peasants becoming quite rich and some poorer and poorer?" (There were becoming available at the time a growing number of reports containing what are known as the Zemstvo statistics; and the chapter consists in large measure of a careful, critical review of a sizeable number of these reports.) Lenin's answer, to summarize it very briefly, is that the observed "differentiation" of the peasantry into "rich," "middle," and "poor" results from an ongoing transformation of the social relations of production in the Russian countryside. The "middle" stratum (30%) for the most part is what remains of the peasantry proper, those still in the lord-peasant relation of production (in its post-emancipation forms). This stratum (and the social structure it is integral to), however, is progressively being eliminated through the increasing formation of capitalist relations of production between the few (20%), who as a result are becoming a class of small bourgeoisie (the "rich"), and the many (50%), who as a result are becoming a class of rural proletarians (the "poor"). The few increasingly concentrate the means of production in their hands (land, draft animals, implements) and so also the means of subsistence, increasingly engage others to work for them, and increasingly produce "for the market." The many increasingly lose possession and control of means of production, increasingly work for others, increasingly purchase their means of subsistence "on the market." The two seemingly different trends—some becoming rich and others becoming poor—are only the necessarily opposite tendencies produced by the single relational development. Accordingly, what is occurring is not the peasantry's differentiation but its disintegration. And it is this ongoing transformation of the relational structure that brings about, and is in part reflected in, the increasingly unequal distribution of material well-being over rural households, which the Zemstvo reports document.

The data here thus come to the analyst in the form of distributions of features (e.g., amount of land leased) over acting agencies (in this case, households) and not in the form of relational matrices (showing, for example, the lease-from/ rent-to relations among the households of an area). Nevertheless the analyst keeps his attention throughout, not on the acting agencies (households), or on abstract categories ("rich," "peasants," etc.) in which they have been classified, but on the developing relations among them and on the processes integral to those relations and their development. The result is a sustained, comprehensive interpretation not otherwise likely.

A second case in point is the core-periphery relational conception. Here, unfortunately, the end-terms "core" and "periphery" all too often become themselves respective foci of attention, categories in their own right, as it were. And the relation which the joined terms designate slips into the background, sometimes out of sight entirely. When that happens the processes continually reproducing the relation, and hence the relational categories, also drop from sight, and we are left with only the categories, which, as a result, are now mere classificatory terms, neither grounded theoretically nor pro-ductive analytically.

Capital accumulation, concentration, and centralization (through the "broadening" as well as the "deepening" of capitalist development, to use Lenin's apposite pairing) are, in the forms in which we know them, the most general and comprehensive of the processes reproducing core-periphery relations (themselves a definite variety of "uneven and com-bined development"). But more immediately related to the conception, as we work with it, is division and integration of labor as processes. For these have as their general direct effect the reproduction and further development of specialized (therefore partial) production-operations—hence, of produc-tion-communities—as distinguishable but not separable production-activities *of* a more or less integrated, continually expanding and deepening world-scale social economy (in that sense, world-economy). Core-periphery relations, or derivatively core-and-periphery formations, are thus, in the first instance, categories of the world-scale social division of labor. Those latter processes, though, are in turn aspects—or better, forms of specification—of the most general and most abstract process, the accumulation of capital (including here the ongoing so-called "primitive" accumulation, i.e., "original" expropriation as a continuing historical process, as well the self-expansion of capital).

Accordingly, to let the relation which "core-and-periphery" designates slip into the background is to let the labor process as it operates on a world scale slip into the background as well. One place in particular where this sort of slippage seems frequently to occur is in discussions of "trade" between "core" and "periphery." With the latter pair as classificatory terms, we say, "Here's a core-country and here's a periphery-country; now, how are they related? Why, through 'trade.'" And with that, a set of activities and interactions we call "trade" ceases to be just one of many ways in which the inter-relations linking the partial-production-operations formative of "cores" and those formative of "peripheries" are actualized, in given times and places. And instead "trade" (almost invariably as "market-trade") becomes *the* form of *the* relationship between *the* core and *the* periphery. We now have two kinds of "things" (world-regions), "cores" and "peripheries," related by (usually) international trade—hence, exchange rates—a world market, terms of trade, and the like. With that the figure-ground inversion is complete, and the basic conception ceases to frame analysis or to guide interpretation.

EXPLANATION AND INTERPRETATION

The second heading under which I want to discuss some issues of method is explanation and interpretation.

Let me turn first to the activity of explaining. As working social scientists, we engage in it all the time; sometimes we do so quite self-consciously, sometimes in a rather off-handed fashion.

Whether or not we are attentive to what we do when we explain, however, may not matter very much. For a particular conception of explaining, seen not as an ongoing activity but as a more or less adequate performance, has become dominant in American philosophical circles—dominant in the sense that, whether you are for that conception or opposed to it, you address yourself to it. This is the "covering law" notion of explanation (Hempel) which, although formulated to facilitate philosophical studies of scientific work, has become, for many social scientists, prescriptive for scientific work.

The nub of the covering-law notion of explanation is exceedingly simple (although after that the idea becomes quite complex). And it looks suspiciously like an elementary syllogism. One wants to explain a described condition, b. This requires a law (one covering the condition) stating, in effect, that if a, then b; it also of course requires an existence statement to the effect that a exists. The full account then consists of statements to the effect that (1) a exists, (2) a law obtains such that if a, then b, and (3) b exists. In this version, the existence statement about a, coupled with the statement of the covering law relating a to b, *together* "explain" b, i.e., logically "produce" (by one calculus or another) the existence statement about b.

This schematic notion of explanation may be useful in summarizing explanatory arguments, as I shall shortly illustrate. It may also, like truth-tables, help to make internally consistent one's own explanatory accounts. But I doubt very much that in itself it is of much help in the actual *activity* of "explaining." For our difficulties lie, not so much in knowing how to cast our interpretive arguments, once they are formulated, as in figuring out how to formulate the arguments in the first place.

But let me first illustrate the claim that interesting explanatory accounts of complex social changes are not necessarily inconsistent with the covering-law formalization of explanation. Let us sketchily restate Lenin's account, mentioned earlier, of why some peasant households were becoming poorer and some richer. The "dependent variable" or, here, the explicandum, is the growing "differentiation of the peasantry" or the increasing inequality of well-being among peasant households. The answer Lenin gave is, in summary, this: new social relations of production are forming among peasant households such that, in relation to one another (and not merely relative to one another), some are becoming small-capitalist households and others proletarian households; such relations presuppose and carry further an unequal distribution over the households of, primarily, means of production and, secondarily, means of subsistence (well-being); the latter inequality constitutes what is seen as the growing "differentiation of the peasantry." Thus we have:

(1) The existence statement that capitalist relations of production are developing in rural Russia;

(2) The law-like statement that the development of capitalist relations of production presupposes and furthers centralization of capital among households and, in addition, an unequal distribution of means of subsistence (well-being) among them;

(3) The derived existence statement is, therefore, that there is an increasing inequality of well-being over peasant households, or a growing differentiation of the peasantry, in rural Russia.

(This is not a particularly precise or elegant version, but it will serve for present purposes.)

How useful is this notion of explanation to working social scientists? My guess is not very (except perhaps in checking out the coherence of one's own, or another's, interpretative argument). Why? Because it presupposes what is at the heart of our working difficulties, namely, how to formulate what seems in need of explanation or interpretation and what laws to use in constructing the explanatory or interpretative account. Or, alternatively, it presupposes laws to work with in seeking to identify what is in need of interpretation and a procedure for moving from the "abstract" law-like formulations to defensible "concrete" interpretative accounts. An analytic philosopher would say, I imagine, that of course such concerns are "presupposed"; they are substantive matters, and we can have nothing of import to say about such things. Which is exactly the first point I wish to make under this heading: namely, the "covering-law" conception of "explanation" may provide some guidelines for writing up the results of an inquiry, once they have been obtained; it provides no guidelines whatsoever to the actual conduct of inquiry, "legitimatizing" footnotes to philosophical writings to the apparent contrary notwithstanding. We are, in short, much more on our own here than we may think or than we may have been led to think.

We then have two distinguishable, if in practice invariably highly interrelated, steps under this heading, the selection of problems and the construction of explanations. In the nature of the case, I can do no more than touch on one or two points in connection with each.

Regarding the selection of problems for inquiry, in studies of long-term, large-scale change, let me start somewhat negatively. A practice has grown up, largely the product of our semi-statistical way of imagining problems of inquiry, which we are probably all engaged fully in at one time or another and probably engage in to some extent most of the time. In this practice, one rapidly (sometimes thoroughly—it does not matter) scans a set of "cases" and classifies them either as instances under some general rubric ("revolutions") or as not instances under it. Alternatively, one scans them with a view to uncovering what a subset of them has in common (which becomes the equivalent of the general rubric) and the remainder lack. Have they or have they not had a revolution? Do they or do they not exhibit democracy (or fascism)? Is there or is there not a true national bourgeoisie? Is the peasantry a decisive social force there or is it not? And so forth. One then, almost without thinking about it, inverts the subject and the predicate: one moves from this "case" exhibiting this "condition" to this "condition" having a "case," as an instance. Now, in so moving, one has "abstracted" the condition and made it, in its now categorical form, the focus of attention and inquiry. But what is there to say about "revolutions," "democracies" (or "fascisms"), "true national bourgeoisie," or "socially decisive peasantries?" Not much (just as there is not much to say about "anomie" or "cross-pressures"). And so one invokes the life-saving queries, "Under what conditions does X occur?" or "Given X, what conditions account for its having different effects?" And all manner of "hypotheses," "theories," and doctoral theses are thereby licensed.

From there it is but a small step to rounding up a set of cases; predicating and measuring properties of each; tracking the observed relations among the measurements; checking out the recurrence of the observed relations under various conditions (the analysis of statistical relations); generalizing the observed relations; and concluding with several new laws of the form: for any s, if x, then (probably) y.

From what has been said above about the singularity of the modern world-system as a complex of spatio-temporal processes (social relations), it should be evident that this way of choosing a subject of inquiry—this highly convention-alized, and convenient, practice—is fundamentally inappro-priate in the study of social change from the world-system angle of vision. For at base the practice presumes a degree (quantitative) and a kind (qualitative) of repetition that the construct—"modern world system"—flatly rules out. To focus on certain seemingly similar conditions in various places at various times; to abstract those conditions from their place-time settings; and to inquire, abstractly, into the causes or consequences of the conditions is to proceed precisely in the one way clearly ruled out of court by the world-system or world-historical perspective on social change.

(The preceding is *not* intended to suggest that the presentation of statistical relations, of the sort alluded to, has no place in world-system studies; that would be silly as well as wrong. It is intended to say that the role of such presentations in world-historical studies is decidedly different from their role in ahistorical inquiries, including studies that come under the heading of the sociology of the past. In much current work, they are used to establish general propositions or to disconfirm them. In world-system studies, their role is fundamentally different. They may function to set up a problem for case-by-case examination; or, at the opposite end, they may be used to summarize results from a case-by-case inquiry. But they can never legitimately serve, as they commonly do in much contemporary inquiry, as substitutes for successive detailed studies of each case. It is the a priori elimination of each case's distinctiveness that the world-system's approach rules out, not the claim that there are comparabilities or similarities.)

As to ways in which to choose a problem for inquiry, we are just beginning to learn them. Let me briefly describe two. One is illustrated by Lenin's study, mentioned above. The general format here is "the development of capitalism in . . ." Within that there is a focus, given in that study by its subtitle, "The process of the formation of a home market for large-scale industry." That, in turn, has an origin simultaneously in a general theoretical problem current at the time (and in the place, Russia), concerning "the realization of the product" *and* in an historically specific interpretative problem, "how and in what direction are the diverse aspects of the Russian national economy developing?" Here a definite theoretical-interpretative concern—how to bring into relation (1) a clear but highly general (abstract) theoretical account and (2) a body of apparently pertinent information about economic activities within a particular place over a particular period— organizes the analysis. The study's conclusion, just to be clear on the matter, concerns the plausibility, not of the abstract theoretical argument but of the interpretative argument (regarding "the formation of the home market").

Another is illustrated by Frances Moulder's slim monograph, *Japan, China and the Modern World Economy* (1977). At the time she began work on it in the mid-sixties as a doctoral research project, the accepted query regarding China and Japan was: Why did Japan modernize and China not do so? Which, in its formulation, directed inquiry inward: What was there about "traditional" Japanese society, in contrast to "traditional" Chinese society, that led the one to modernize and the other to fail to? Moulder, working from the world-system perspective, sharply restated the question: How did Japan come to occupy the place it has in the world economy and China to occupy the place it has? Here, then, we have a problem generated, and a line of interpretation suggested, by the world-historical perspective but, in this case, without there being, as well, a governing general theoretical problem (such as the "realization problem"). More generally, perhaps, studies of the development of capitalism that are oriented to its "deepening," such as Lenin's, may be more explicitly theoretically oriented to begin with than studies of its development oriented to its "broadening," owing to the scope and limiting assumptions of *Capital*. Moulder subtitles her study, "Toward a reinterpretation of East Asian development ca. 1600 to ca. 1918." We shall probably need a number of such polemically framed interpretative works before a *theory* of noncapitalist expansion of capital, comparable in generality to and integrated with the theory of the self-expansion of capital, can be stated sufficiently fully and abstractly to serve as the guide to orienting *theoretical* problems.

I now turn to the last topic, the construction of explanations. Two matters concern me here, the first being the use of "laws" in interpretative accounts. Christopher Chase-Dunn (Chapter 6 in this volume) sketched a set of law-like statements. The construction of such arguments-in-the-abstract is an indispensable step in inquiry and a needed intermediate activity we all should engage in. But Chase-Dunn was also worried about "testing" his interpretation-sketch. And that I have misgivings about.

For he may have meant: constructing Hempel-like rules of interpretation linking his concepts to indicators of them; making (obtaining) the thereupon requisite kinds of observations (measurements) and examining the observable patterns among interrelated arrays; and "concluding" from all this that his interpretation-sketch is warranted, in some general sense, by this sequence of activities or made abstractly plausible by it. For if that is what he did mean by "testing," then in the light of what I have been saying, I evidently think he is on the wrong track. I do not know that that is what Chase-Dunn meant; I only want to express my misgivings if it *is* what he meant.

It seems to me that Richard Rubinson (Chapter 2 in this volume) carried a Chase-Dunn-like argument in the direction it should go, that is, he puts a general argument to use in (for a short paper) a reasonably specific way in order to interpret ("explain") a particular development. Both the U.S. and Germany, he observes, became core powers in about the same period. From a world-system perspective (more specifically, assuming *some* proportionality in core-periphery relations), this "expansion" of the core-arena of the system would seem to entail (imply) an "expansion" of the periphery-arena. This he can document, and he then turns to the related processes through which center-coalitions both form within the two core-area jurisdictions under discussion and proceed, simultaneously with the system's "expansion," to develop relatively strong state structures (or, better, processes). I don't think the method here is at all mystical. He moves toward his subject matter, making tactical use of contradictions in his exposition, in what seems to me a rather sound scientific fashion.

I do, however, miss one important kind of consideration in his account, and noting that will wind up these comments. I have in mind the relation between "internal" contradictions and "external" contradictions. Specifically, I could detect no connection, in the account as given here by Rubinson, between the balance of forces (processes) accounting for center-coalition formation and expansion and the balance of forces (processes) accounting for core-arena (and therefore periphery-arena) expansion. That seems to me an analytic weakness in the account as given; I do not think our rules of procedure permit us *this* kind of incompleteness in our accounts.

I want to conclude, with an illustration of the point, by bringing these two sets of contradictions into relation with one another in the course of constructing explanatory accounts, but I shall have to reach for a far-removed example. (Mao's essay "on contradiction" sketches the general, schematic considerations more fully than any other single source I know.) At the time the British were forming a colonial unit they would call Uganda, there was in what became that colony's southwest corner a centrally organized "kingdom," Ankole. Internal to this kingdom were many tensions, among which two are pertinent here. One was between the Omugabe ("king") and his clan brothers (the "aristocracy"), each of whom was by birth if not by events as qualified as the incumbent to rule. Another was between these "princes of the drum," collectively, and the powerful, but by clan ineligible, "commoner" chiefs. In the century preceding the establishment of British overrule, both had come to be dominant tensions within the kingdom, for the incumbent kings had worked successfully with the commoner chiefs to strengthen considerably the "royal" power at the expense of the aristocratic power, and hence to strengthen commoner chiefly power against aristocratic chiefly power. Externally, the kingdom was under pressure from several sides, one of which was the kingdom of Buganda. The British then appeared, on the side of Buganda (itself a complicated story), altering the balance of forces "externally." The second in command in the kingdom, as it were, who was a commoner, made arrangements with the Baganda and the British, altering the balance of forces "internally." Then, as overrule took effect through the Omugabe and (primarily) the commoner chiefs, the pressures on the aristocratic chiefs grew, and eventually they fled, fundamentally altering the balance of forces ("contradictions") within the now-incorporated kingdom. Coupled with this was the formation of Uganda, and so a whole structurally new set of "internal" and "external" contradictions began to form (and mature). Or at least—and this is the point, of course—that is one way of beginning to organize an account of the establishment/elaboration of imperial overrule in one particular instance. More generally, perhaps, anti-overrule begins with overrule; or, anti-imperialism with imperialism.

So far as constructing interpretative accounts is concerned, we have barely begun to appreciate the power of the "internal"/ "external" sets of contradictions—let alone sketch a "logic" for them.

Chapter 9

WORLD-SYSTEM ANALYSIS:
THEORETICAL AND INTERPRETATIVE ISSUES

Immanuel Wallerstein

If we start with the elementary premise that everything is process, then we have a problem of discourse, which runs as follows: The only way we can talk about process is to utilize categories, which must, in fact, reflect some kind of patterns that we think are repeated over some period of time or space. But we simultaneously talk about the same process as though, in fact, it were continuous *development*; that is, a continuous change in every one of those patterns, a structural transformation. There is, then, a fundamental antinomy in our language.

In explaining the world-system perspective we may begin with a pair of terms called core and periphery. This pair of terms has been around for 25 years and comes out of the U.N. Economic Commission on Latin America in the late 1940s and early 1950s. These two terms are nouns, but they are also adjectives. As soon as you think of them as adjectives, however, you wonder what nouns the adjectives get attached to.

There is a certain sloppiness of which I myself have been guilty, and which I see repeatedly, of not worrying about the fact that we use the same adjectives for different nouns.

For example, we talk of core areas or core zones, peripheral areas and peripheral zones. We talk of core processes and peripheral processes; we talk of core products and peripheral products. And then perhaps the most important confusion is that we talk of core states and peripheral states.

There lies behind this a theoretical problem, which we have to wrestle with and I do not have any easy answers. It derives from the lack of total coincidence between the economic processes and the state boundaries. If one starts with the framework of a single division of labor within which there are multiple states and multiple economic processes, then one has to worry about the lack of total coincidence.

The interrelationship and the interaction between the core processes and the states in which they are located, the fact of multiple layers of coreness and peripherality, get at the fact that there exist sets of dyadic relationships, within dyadic relationships within dyadic relationships and overlapping dyadic relationships, which are by no means simple to sort out in the actual analysis.

Obviously if we start with core and periphery—and I leave out semi-periphery quite purposely for the moment—what are we talking about? Well, we are talking about some kind of related set of production processes which are unequal; between their products there is unequal exchange. Now unequal exchange is a very contentious topic. The term was formulated by Emmanuel (1972), who was attempting to refute the notion that the process of international trade was beneficial to both sides, in the classic statement of Ricardo. I want to demonstrate in a kind of rigorous logical fashion that trade within a capitalist world-system is inherently unequal. This raises the question as to whether there is another kind of exchange which is equal, and I want to come back to that in a moment. What, in fact, do we mean by unequal exchange? It is something in addition to the fact that there is a transfer of surplus value from a direct producer to another person who, by one legal means or another, obtains that surplus.

Now unequal exchange refers to something over and above that. In addition to that, if there are two *pairs* of producers and receivers of surplus-value, Emmanuel is arguing that the receiver of one pair acquires part of the surplus-value *of the other pair*. This is, of course, not given at the expense of the producer of the second pair, because he has already given up his surplus-value, but rather is given up at the expense of that receiver. This relationship is what we are talking about when we refer to core-periphery.

Emmanuel gives an explanation of the origins of that relationship in which he argues that it comes from differential wage rates historically determined. I do not want to review the debate involved here, but I want to emphasize the fact that unequal exchange is over and above the simple transfer of surplus-value from the direct producer to the person who immediately receives it.

Part of Emmanuel's explanation depends upon the fact that the exchange has crossed the national boundary, and that may or may not be essential. It seems to me that it is not and that, in fact, one could make the case that trade within states between rural and urban areas is also a trade of unequal exchange.

Surplus-value, once created, gets distributed among a large number of people beyond the person who first obtains that segment of created value. In the whole circuit of capital that value may get distributed to a multiplicity of people. And the core-periphery relationship indicates the degree to which surplus-value is unevenly distributed in the direction of the core. What we are talking about now is a process. The degree to which the economic relationship is core-peripheralized is the degree to which there is an increasingly unequal distribution of the surplus product between two different bourgeoisies.

Now how does that relate to states? We discover a pattern in which core-type activities and peripheral-type activities are unequally geographically distributed across the world-system and within segments of the world-system. There are concentrations, for good reasons, of core-like activities within particular areas. And since state lines are drawn arbitrarily by any means and are constantly redrawn, we can in fact make calculations for any given time of the sum of the nature of activities within the state boundaries. And we will discover, if we do that, that areas we normally refer to as peripheral areas are areas where the vast majority of activity would, in fact, come into the category of peripheral activity. But in areas which have many core activities it is *not* necessarily the case that the *vast majority* of activities are core activities. Core states tend to have peripheral activities as well.

Where then, does semi-periphery come in? I and others have insisted that there is this third category. It is obviously quite different. It is not an economic activity because this is a *dyadic* relationship of unequal exchange between a *pair* of objects that are exchanged in the division of labor.

Semi-peripheral seems to be almost by definition an adjective you apply to states as opposed to core and periphery. A semi-peripheral state appears to be a state which has a roughly even balance of core-like and peripheral-like activity. This has, of course, important political consequences. The model of a semi-peripheral state is the one that exports the peripheral products to core countries and core products to peripheral areas of the world-system and does both in roughly equivalent degrees. I would like to underline the apparent theoretical symmetry of this whole process.

That, then, gets us to the issue of states and their roles. Fred Block (Chapter 1 in this volume) talked about it in terms of reproaching me for not being sufficiently "structural," that I allowed intentionality to creep in at least for the core zones. I have had the opposite criticism, and I like his better. Obviously intentionality does not have to be expressed always in explicit statements or actions. Intentionality only has to be overtly expressed if it is necessary to express it. If things are, in fact, going along the way one wishes, one does not have to *intend* to do things. One can allow things to simply occur. Second, the contrast which he drew was not between intentionality and nonintentionality, but between short-run and long-run intentionality, the economic managers having more short-run intentionality. Up to a point, I would buy this generalization, and the man who makes that generalization best and most convincingly is Schumpeter in *Capitalism, Socialism, and Democracy* (1942), where he draws the distinction between the ruling feudal strata of the capitalist system and the bourgeoisie who need them because they cannot think in those ways and because they cannot manage states.

I raised the question that if there is *unequal* exchange, is there also *equal* exchange? And what would equal exchange mean? If unequal exchange means, ultimately, the transfer of some of the surplus of one area to a receiver of surplus in another, this is the consequence of the fact that more labor power has gone into producing the value exchanged in one area than in the other.

An equal exchange might conceivably mean two possible things. Either equal labor is being exchanged, which is the kind of Ricardian model, or value*less* things are being exchanged, i.e., valueless as determined on each end, but, of course, valuable as determined on the other end. That is not a totally fictitious situation. I will come back to that in terms of the external arena.

The first theoretical problem is how we are going to formulate the process of peripheral*ization* in relationship to states, which momentarily and temporarily have differential amounts of these activities located within them and, therefore, have difference kinds of politics which we might talk about as core, semi-peripheral, and peripheral states.

The second kind of theoretical problem relates to the class struggle or class structure. Douglas Dowd (Chapter 7 in this volume) made a great show at being a heretic, so in the best tradition of "can you top this?" I thought the only thing I could do to beat that was to make a great show of being

orthodox. I think the most unorthodox thing that most orthodox
Marxists do is that, when they talk about class conflict, they
do not really take it seriously.

I think the one insight that Marx had most clearly and most
correctly about class relations and capitalism—but, I hasten
to add, he really never wrote about it in any serious way—
was that there is a process of polarization, a *process* of the
creation of *two* classes. I would like to take that very seriously.
I would like to suggest that the insight is correct, that over
historical time there has in fact been an increasing polarization,
which is the consequence of two processes—proletarianization
and bourgeoisification—in capitalism. That is the essence of
the capital-labor relationship.

I think we can now handle surplus-value in a way that will
make Dowd happy, if not others. If you take the ideal-type
of proletarian, and most Marxists are very Weberian in the
way they use ideal-types, he is the image of the 1820-1830
English factory worker straight from the rural areas, who,
one generation back, has been pushed off the land, who has
no other source of income, who is living in a miserable hovel,
who is working 16-18 hours a day, and who is receiving through
the iron law of wages the minimum wage it takes to reproduce
him.

If one looks for this ideal-type household, one which has
no other source of lifetime income except the wages which
the household receives from employers in return for work,
and if one adds the requirement that the wages be in fact
sufficient for the household to subsist over life, then the
number of cases that fall within this category are incredibly
small, although there are probably more today than there
were 100 or 200 years ago.

These people, even in a core country, do not make up
anywhere near the majority of a country's population. In fact,
a large portion of the workforce of the world, not merely in
the 16th century, but also in the year 1977, are, to use a very
long phrase, what I would call part-lifetime proletarian

households or incomplete proletarians. What I mean is the following: The largest bulk of workers do not receive their entire lifetime income from the employer. They also receive money from two other possible sources. One is the work that they themselves do; for example, the wife cooks. That is work, and it reduces the cost of subsistence, because the wife is not hiring someone else to do it. But if I leave aside my extreme example and take a more readily acceptable one, there is the garden plot, generically speaking, that is the direct production of food in some way. This is a very widespread phenomenon. Even Pittsburgh steel workers engaged in this type of activity just 40 years ago, and if you look for this in the world-system as a whole, and you remember that we are calculating this over a lifetime, you begin to see we are talking of a very large group indeed.

Now let me add the second source. In addition to the income this household receives in wages and the income in kind that they themselves produce, through one mechanism or another, there is also gift income: in the Third World, the cousin who gives part of his income to the family; in the USA, the parent who supports his children. In fact, such gift income is widespread.

That is not unimportant for the following reasons. There are two processes that affect the overall wage levels. Process number one is that of inserting people into the world-economy, or peripheralization. It involves taking a household which at T_1 is outside the world-economy and 20 years later is inside. Peripheralization means, first of all, a significant reduction in real income for households. The process of pauperization, which is talked about somewhat metaphorically in the Marxist corpus, refers to this process. This process is not minor but terribly significant, and could be drawn on a scale over time such that you would come up with figures showing a downward trend. This involves all these people of whom I use this awkward phrase, part-lifetime proletarian households. I would then suggest that the transition of individual households to full-lifetime proletarian household status would represent for the individual household an *increase* in real income. The opposite image found in Marx and particularly in Engels is totally wrong. Going from that rural area in the 18th century to that urban area in the 19th century was not a reduction in income for the individual family, but, in fact, an increase, and that increase has continued ever since.

This then is Dowd's problem. I agree with what he was saying, but I did not like the way he formulated the working class. What he means is that these people, who get more real income than the vast majority of the world's population, are not the miserable bottom of the world and have reflected class interests in being social-democrats. And this is perfectly explicable through economistic categories. They are not the lowest level of the world and they are disproportionately represented in core countries, which explains, within the Skocpol-Trimberger formulations, no revolutions in the core but only in the Third World. I am not sure we want to accept that fully, but it does have some realities.

It is important to see the process as a continuum from being totally outside the world-economy to inclusion within the lowest possible level (an inclusion which, by definition, in order for it to be at the lowest possible level, must not involve full-lifetime wage labor), to inclusion at a "higher" level, via the internal processes of capitalism which force some of these families over time to be promoted to the status of full-time proletarians.

That the full-lifetime proletarian receives a higher wage than the part-lifetime holds on the assumption that we are now dealing with an unskilled household, which is receiving *no more* than the minimum wage.

That is to say, if the employer pays the man over a lifetime, or a household over its lifetime, the amount which is required to sustain them in life is the physiologically minimum wage. However, if a cousin can sustain a family for part of a lifetime, or if the household itself can sustain *itself* for part of a lifetime, it is possible for the employer to pay for that portion of the life in which this household works for the employer, less the proportionate amount of a lifetime minimum wage.

This is the basic explanation for the differential in the same work, in different parts of the world, receiving vastly different wage rates. This can be explained because workers in many parts of the world are part-time proletarians and can be given wages *below* the physiological minimum wage.

Incidentally that explains why it is essential to the functioning of the capitalist system that everybody not be a proletarian. In fact, the mixture of wage and nonwage labor is the essence of capitalism. Indeed one of the contradictions of capitalism is the process of proletarianization, which is a process that cuts into the process of capital accumulation.

Bourgeoisification presents similar issues, and this is why I say most "orthodox" Marxists do not take it seriously. If they really took the concept of polarization seriously, they would not be asking questions all the time about all these other categories—aristocrats, landowners—who are narrowly defined as outside the bourgeoisie.

I think again the one thing I absolutely agree with in what Dowd said is that the heart of the issue is the process of accumulation. What makes for the bourgeoisification of a man, who controls production in any fashion, is the degree to which he tends to act in terms of accumulating surplus. After all, the essence of capitalism is that surplus is accumulated, not just received. It is accumulated systematically, and it is an expanding system. The transformation of people who are oriented to expending the surplus, rather than accumulating it, is a structural process in which the individuals involved are forced in that direction. Nobody ever does it perfectly; there is no ideal bourgeois, but there are some who are more bourgeois than others. Over time, more and more are forced by the process of the competitive market, which weeds out those who refuse to operate within a capitalist framework in function of the imperatives of accumulation.

Now that does not mean that, at any given time, many people, even most people, do not act in a contrary fashion. But every time we talk about the centralization of capital, what on earth do we mean except that the guys who are more bourgeois beat out the guys who are less bourgeois and they are the ones who centralize capital? As a result, the others lose out. It may take a generation, it may take six generations for them to lose out; but, again, it is a process.

So there is no proletariat, no bourgeoisie; *a fortiori*, these are not adjectives for states. What on earth could it mean to call a place a bourgeois state? Or a proletarian state? These are economic categories. And they are processes over historical time, which over time are going to transform the system into something which it is not.

That then gets us into politics. Walter Goldfrank (Chapter 3 in this volume) asked what is a primary contradiction as opposed to a secondary one. I have a provisional answer I want to try on you. If we say that the capitalist world-system is a system of polarization of classes—proletarianization, on the one hand, and bourgeoisification, on the other—then there are two kinds of politics. There are the politics that are *between* these two emerging groups, and then there are the politics *within* those groups.

If you were to sit down and do a content analysis of books of history, to see if political conflicts were between classes or within classes, I think you would find on any rapid checklist that you did that about 95% of the conflicts within the world are in fact *within* classes. This is so for battles for control of state structure, electoral battles, economic battles, street battles, military battles. Such conflicts are much more frequent, although not more important, than in*ter*-class battles.

Of course, in reality, any large-scale battle mixes the two. If you look at the French Revolution, or the English Revolution, or any major event that goes on over a number of years, obviously and concretely they will mix up these two kinds of battles. Let us come to primary and secondary contradictions.

As a first stab, maybe what we mean is that *inter*-class battles are the primary contradictions and *intra*-class battles are the secondary ones, although again the secondary are numerically larger. Since this is not a simple dyadic relationship, but rather layers within layers within layers, then it becomes a complicated situation.

But do not forget my unequal exchange where a bourgeois in one area may be gaining an advantage over a bourgeois in another area as well as the proletarian of his own area. As a result there may be an intra-class battle which may take the form of economic nationalism, or even national liberation movements, as well as inter-class struggles.

Let us go on to a third theoretical issue, to which we also do not have easy answers. If periphery is not a state but a process, then we have the noun peripheralization. This refers to two things, to use that old logical pair—extensive and intensive.

Intensive refers to the degree to which, once you have a dyadic relationship between a core process and peripheral process, it might tilt in a more unequal direction. We could call that a deepening of peripheralization, and surely that happens all the time. But extensive refers to the inclusion of a unit, or an area which was not previously involved at all, into the functioning world-economy. For this, we use the phrase peripheralization.

The minute we think of it in this way we have a problem of boundaries. If we say a world-economy is an entity that has an effective ongoing integration of division of labor, then we have to know what is included—physically and economically—in that division of labor. In fact, as it turns out, I would again like to reformulate something that Dowd said earlier. He stated that the world-economy and capitalism did not really get going until the late 19th century, which makes a difference as to how it functions. The historical points earlier than that add up to an area smaller than the entire world. But this area, in fact, was expanding over time. There are reasons why it expanded, and obviously it can only expand to the limit. This process of expansion is a part of the process of peripheralization. I would say for instance, that India (or at least parts of India) was peripheralized in the late 18th or early 19th centuries. Prior to that point, although it was engaged in trade, the trade between India and 17th-century Europe is not part of capitalism. But trade in the 19th century between England and India was part of capitalism, and that is what one means by the peripheralization of India. It is a transition from being an external arena to being a peripheral area within the world capitalist system.

Incidentally, this means a fall of real income of direct producers in India. I would contend that a careful study would show that in the year 1900 direct producers in India received significantly less for comparable types of work than they did in 1600. And that is the immiserization process caused by the incorporation within the capitalist world-system.

The theoretical problem is how do we know these boundaries. I make the statement that, as of 1750 or 1765, India began to be included into the world-economy. Before that it was not. You would want to know why it was not. On an empirical basis, it is a very difficult question, but it is even difficult on the theoretical level. What kind of criteria are we, in fact, going to use to determine this? And that gets us into the whole question of equal and unequal trade and luxuries. Luxuries are an important concept. The most important evidence to show this is that people talk as though they were. In the early modern era, there were such external arenas. There was then actually a word for the trade of luxuries which every trader knew. It was called the rich trades. This was seen to be very different from the other kinds of trade. The only place where this is theoretically developed is in Sraffa (1972) and I direct you to that book. Let me give you a layman's version of that point. I think the essence of a rich trade is a trade between A-B in which the producers of A think that they are giving B something utterly worthless; the producers of B think they are giving A something worthless; however, each thinks they are receiving something marvelous.

It seems improbable on the face of it. So read carefully the descriptions of this kind of trade—I have done this in relation to Africa—and you will see that such pairs of attitudes *did* exist.

The determination of boundaries I think is extremely important. It gets into the whole question that Richard Rubinson (Chapter 2 in this volume) raises, as his whole analysis hinges on the expansion of outer boundaries, which created "rule." So we cannot even take his interpretation and say does it make any sense, unless we can translate, in some empirical way, the concept of boundaries and see whether there was more room in the middle of the 19th century than there had been 50, 70, or 100 years earlier. Thus, we have to worry about equal and unequal exchange as processes and what luxuries might mean. We are also going to have to worry about inner boundaries, because, if we look at it in the very early stages, there exists a set of outer boundaries, but there are also *inner* areas that are not involved. The political processes of incorporating inner areas into larger economic areas are obscure, and we have to worry about how we will define them.

I would like now to make a distinction between the true subsistence farmer, who, although on a map, he looks like he is part of the world-economy, is in fact outside it, and the man living in a rural area, who spends most of his time making food for himself, but also sends out his cousin to the urban area (or to some other rural area to work on a cash crop), and is supplying part of a surplus which is enabling the mine-owner or other employer to pay that cousin his total income. He is *not* a subsistence worker. He is *not* outside the world-economy. He is producing real surplus, which is in fact fed right into the world-economy and ends up in the counting houses in London or Amsterdam.

Now we get to the last theoretical problem, and that comes back to my very first point, which is that everything is process. But we have to worry about modes of discourse, patterns which are repeated, and development which changes all the time, and that gets translated into two large-scale things that occur within the world-economy, which I would summarize as cyclical rhythms and secular trends.

The cyclical rhythms are the things that more or less seem to repeat themselves over time. The secular trends are those processes which are in some sense linear. Of course, a cyclical trend never perfectly repeats itself, but more or less does. Now, there are two issues here, but, even if we know how to distinguish the two, how do the two intermix? They go on side by side simultaneously, which is very important. I think the cyclical rhythms are these long waves, which people are discovering and rediscovering today. Mandel, who has been mentioned several times, and others are doing so. There has also been a long history of *observation* that there are "expansions" and "contractions" in the world-economy in one form or another. I think they are linked to a basic contradiction of the system, which has to do with supply and demand, that is, *world-system* supply and world-system demand, not *firm* supply and demand, nor *state* supply and demand, but world-system supply and demand.

We talk about the contradiction of social production and the anarchy of distribution. But there is another contradiction, which is that production decisions—that is, supply decisions— are in fact anarchic. That is to say, they are in the hands of dispersed producers, each of whom is always operating in the short-term interest of maximizing profits and optimizing it. This means that he competes with others, so that these people may overproduce, because each believes they are producing for a particular market. Demand decisions, however, are sociopolitically given. That is, distribution at any historical epoch is according to an effective worldwide political compromise, which operates and determines the historically given wage levels, which of course vary, but within ranges.

I think the pattern of the cyclical rhythm is related to the world effective demand. At any given point it is a certain level. Expansion in the world-economy means that more and more producers are producing more and more, finally exceeding world effective demand. There are two basic ways to increase world effective demand. One is the expansion of the boundaries of the system, outer and inner. The other way is a renegotiation of historically given wages that takes the form, I would contend, of transforming a part of the incomplete proletariat into complete proletarians. This means an effective real increase in income, which therefore effectively increases world demand, but at the expense of some profit levels, because these workers are getting paid more.

So you have a dynamic here which explains proletarianization, which is now the first of the secular trends. I have given you, in fact, two secular trends of the world-system. One is expansion, the second is proletarianization. A third is commodification, a fourth is mechanization, a fifth is political organization —which others have raised.

I will not go into detail about these latter trends but let me indicate what they have in common. Systemic secular trends are all defined in terms of percentages. And anything you define in percentage has an asymptote. It cannot go on forever. It is logically impossible to talk about 105% of the land area of the world-economy, for example.

You then have to ask the question: What are the dynamics of the contradictions of the system? The dynamics are that the cyclical rhythms, which are the consequence of the structure of capitalism as a system—(i.e., anarchic production and socially determined demand), as mechanisms to resolve the regular mini-crises that this creates, force secular transformations of the system, which are the secular trends that are asymptotic and which, when they reach a certain level, make the system unfunctional, because it would be impossible at that point to have the further continuing of accumulation of capital. You could only cut into the effective distribution of the surplus, which would push logically into an egalitarian route.

So if you ask an optimism-pessimism question, I am coming out very much on the structural side. And part of that structure is the political organization of anti-systemic forces. We have to ask who would have interests that would, in fact, push them to be anti-systemic. And then we find a lot of different types, and it is not necessarily the case that skilled workers in core countries are very high on this category even though they have grievances. A lot of people have grievances, however, that do not push them in anti-systemic directions, but only momentarily push them. They have grievances, but they perhaps have less grievances than a lot of other people such as oppressed ethnic groups in core countries or peasantries in Third World countries.

Obviously, when you put together, in a multi-layered complex system in which there are constant repetitions of dyadic unequal relations, people who push against the system, then you put together a very diverse group. Two things can be said. Any particularly defined group may only momentarily be anti-systemic and then they get their part of the pie and get co-opted. But then there are always new groups, who, for various reasons, are getting into a position of having enough consciousness to act in an anti-systemic manner. I believe this to be a cumulative process, because I think the contradictions are in fact getting greater. In the 17th century, how many significant anti-systemic forces can we count up? There were isolated peasant revolts here, and food riots there. But they were hardly anti-systemic. In the 19th century, we get labor movements, socialist parties, and the beginnings of nationalisms. But in the 20th century we have the Russian Revolution, the Chinese Revolution, and Black Power in the U.S., and some or most may be co-opted out, but the sum total is increasing.

There is a continuing class struggle not only within the states that are governed by socialist parties, but within the parties themselves. It is meaningful to talk about a capitalist-roader, and a socialist-roader, within the parties. It reflects very real differences in socioeconomic interests. A Chinese bureaucrat is in power for 20 years. Then you are faced with the following real question. If China engages in orienting its productive activities for commodity exchange on a world market, the consequence will be that, over the next 20 years, a certain number of goods will flow in and be distributed such that, over those 20 years, the cadres will be more likely to live at a significantly higher income level than if they do not do that.

You may then rationally—intellectually—lecture to them. You may say that it will delay by 46 years the coming of communist utopia, but this cadre has a structural motivation to be a capitalist-roader. He may overcome it, through will and ideology, but I think there was a healthy skepticism on Mao's part about the efficacy of ideology countering in the long-run structural forces. You cannot rely on these people's beliefs remaining at a level such that they will be ready to work against their self-interests. What you can rely upon is organizing other people with opposite self-interests, within China, within the Soviet Union, within the U.S. Now, obviously, you have to look for the forces who have opposite interests. That other individuals, by ideology, may join those forces is, of course, continually possible, but it is not the base of a long-run movement.

REFERENCES

EMMANUEL, A. (1972). Unequal exchange. New York: Monthly Review Press.
SCHUMPETER, J.A. (1942). Capitalism, socialism, and democracy. New York: Harper.
SRAFFA, P. (1972). Production of commodities by means of commodities. Cambridge: Cambridge University Press.

NOTES ON THE CONTRIBUTORS

FRED BLOCK is in the Sociology Department, University of Pennsylvania, and is currently at the Institute of International Studies, University of California, Berkeley. His related writings include *The Origins of International Economic Disorder: American International Monetary Policy since 1941* (1977), and "Contradictions of Capitalism as a World System," *Insurgent Sociologist* (1975).

WALTER F. CARROLL is a Ph.D. candidate in sociology at the American University and a member of the Middle East Research Information Project. He is currently engaged in a comparative study of state capitalism in the Middle East.

CHRISTOPHER CHASE-DUNN teaches in the Department of Social Relations, the Johns Hopkins University. He is publishing "Toward a structural perspective on the world-system" with Richard Rubinson in John. W. Meyer and Michael T. Hannan, eds. *National Development and the World System*, forthcoming.

DOUGLAS DOWD has taught at Berkeley, Cornell, and University of California at Santa Cruz. He is currently at San Jose State College. He has written extensively on capitalism, including *The Twisted Dream: Capitalist Development in the United States since 1776.*

SAMIH K. FARSOUN is in the Sociology Department at the American University and is a member of the Middle East Research Information Project. With Barbara Hockey Kaplan he has been developing a graduate program in political, economic, and historical sociology. He has written extensively on the Middle East.

WALTER L. GOLDFRANK is Associate Professor of Sociology at the University of California, Santa Cruz. He has written extensively on the Mexican Revolution.

TERENCE K. HOPKINS is Director of Graduate Studies, Sociology Department, State University of New York at Binghamton, and has a work in progress on issues of method in the study of historical change.

BARBARA HOCKEY KAPLAN teaches at American University. She arranged the program for the 1977 Spring Conference on the Political Economy of the World System, together with Walter Carroll and Samih Farsoun, with whom she is developing the graduate program in macrosociology. Related writing is on colonialism and nationalism in South East Asia.

RICHARD RUBINSON teaches in the Department of Social Relations, the Johns Hopkins University. In addition to an article with Chase-Dunn, presenting their structural perspective on the world-system, he has published "The world-economy and the distribution of income within states" in the *American Sociological Review* (1976) and "Dependence, government revenue, and economic growth, 1955-1970," *Studies in Comparative International Development* (1977).

THEDA R. SKOCPOL teaches in the Social Studies Program, Harvard University. Her book *States and Social Revolutions in France, Russia, and China* is being published by the Cambridge University Press. Her essay review, "Wallerstein's World Capitalist System: A Theoretical and Historical Critique," appeared in the *American Journal of Sociology* (March 1977).

ELLEN KAY TRIMBERGER teaches at Sonoma State College. Her related writings include *Revolution from Above: Military Bureaucrats and Modernization in Japan, Turkey, Egypt and Peru* (1977) and "State power and modes of production: implications of the Japanese transition to capitalism," *Insurgent Sociologist* (1977).

IMMANUEL WALLERSTEIN is Distinguished Professor of Sociology and Director of the Fernand Braudel Center for the Study of Economies, Historical Systems and Civilizations at the State University of New York at Binghamton. In addition to *The Modern World System*, which was awarded the Sorokin Prize in 1975, his recent books include: *World Inequality* (1975), *Political Economy of Contemporary Africa,* co-edited with Peter C. Gutkind (1976), and *The Capitalist World-Economy* (forthcoming).